EVAI

INS

Papers Prese
Evalu

Library of Congress Catalog Card No. 75-677
ISBN 0-87650-062-9

LIBR

PIERIAN PRESS
P.O. Box 1808
Ann Arbor, Michigan 48106

Contents

tational, programs. While the distinction between orientation and instructional activity is admittedly difficult to recognize in certain instances, the term "orientation" is used here to refer to the familiarization of students to the geographical arrangement of the library and the term "instruction" to refer tot he teaching of the use of library tools, either singularly or in aggregate. As orientation programs tend to be comparatively straightforward in their objectives and approach, it was felt that the more complex instructional activities presented the most serious problems for the evaluator.

The opening paper heard by the conference, presented by Thomas Kirk, defines and examines the need for evaluating programs of library instruction and reviews the past research in the field. Mr. Kirk is Science Librarian at Earlham College in Richmond, Indiana, and is Chairman of the ACRL Bibliographic Instruction Task Force. His work in library instruction, particularly his 1971 *College and Research Libraries* study comparing two methods of library instruction, is well known. As a "state of the art" report on the evaluation of library instruction, the Kirk paper is unique and overdue.

The second conference paper, authored by Richard R. Johnson, Program Manager for the Exxon Education Foundation, concerns the methodology of evaluation and the application of this methodology to library instruction. Dr. Johnson's academic training is in the field of psychology, a discipline notably more at ease with the topic of evaluation than is librarianship, and his introduction to the topic of library instruction came while he was on the psychology faculty at Earlham College. Dr. Johnson's entertaining approach to what is for many a somewhat frightening topic made this presentation one of the most popular of the conference.

The following papers by Trish Culkin, Betty Hacker and Richard Stevens, John Lubins, and Marvin Wiggins were presented in a panel discussion of evaluation case–studies. Each of these writers enjoys a national or regional reputation for their work in the field of bibliographic instruction and the descriptions of their evaluative re– search will be of benefit to others beginning similar undertakings. As is usually the case in this type of panel discussion, many pertinent questions were raised by the audience concerning each presentation and the editor regrets that acoustical and technical problems made the inclusion of these questions and remarks impossible. However, appearing before the Wiggins' paper are the critical remarks made by Rowena Swanson of the University of Denver Graduate School of Librarianship, who sat on the panel with the other five participants. Dr. Swanson was asked to comment extemporaneously on the evaluations discussed and she performed this task with her usual clarity and sharpness, providing an appreciated contribution to the conference and to this collection.

In closing, the editor wishes to thank each of the conference speakers, not only for their excellent presentations, but for their much needed advice and support as well; and to extend a special thanks to Hannelore Rader, Orientation Librarian at Eastern Michigan University for agreeing to make the closing address on extremely short notice. In recognition of the crucial role which they played in all aspects of the conference preparations, I would also like to thank my colleagues at the University of Denver Libraries for their able assistance, kind direction, and unbelievable patience.

Denver
October 29, 1974

BIBLIOGRAPHIC INSTRUCTION – A REVIEW OF RESEARCH

Thomas Kirk
Science Librarian
Earlham College

It is often said that there has not been much research done on the topic of evaluation, and yet when one begins to look into the literature and to talk to people, one finds a great deal of material which discusses a greater and greater number of problems and issues. This paper will review the question of why to evaluate bibliographic instruction programs, this enlarging body of material on bibliographic instruction research, and what needs to be done in the near future. The definition which I will be using is that library instruction evaluation is a systematic collection of data to determine as precisely as possible the cause and effect relationships amongst student backgrounds, bibliographic instruction programs, library use, and student attitudes toward the library.

POSITIVE RESULTS OF EVALUATION

Evaluation improves library instruction, not just in the obvious way that presumably the evaluation will show whether students are becoming more effective library users, but in many indirect ways which we tend to ignore. The first one, inherent in the definition that I have given, is the idea of a systematic data collection. We too often, like faculty members, tend to base our evaluation of an instructional program simply on the basis of the random comments of vocal students. Librarians need to make a systematic collection of data which will have the advantage of getting greater feedback from all types of students.

A second set of benefits of evaluation result from attention to objectives. Some people might claim that you do not really have to establish objectives; you can simply give instruction and then administer a test to check on how well the students have learned what has been taught. On the contrary, we should recognize that the test items are our objectives. We should recognize that the objectives are going to be there whether or not we consciously decide what they are going to be. Therefore we should try to state our objectives

1

before we start and not rationalize them after the fact. Objectives also have the advantage that they focus on the learning process and not on the teaching. When you start writing objectives and start testing a student on his accomplishments, you begin to look primarily at what he or she has done, not solely at what you as a teacher have done. Another side benefit of objectives is the focus on attitudes as well as content. While evaluating, one becomes aware that the students' attitudes towards the instruction, towards the library, and towards the library staff are very important.

A third benefit of evaluation is that it provides a method, or vehicle, for accountability in the management of libraries. The whole question of reference service in the academic library and how it can be managed properly is a question that is receiving more attention, as is the question of whether or not library instruction is an efficient way of providing that reference service. The evaluation of library instruction programs will help explain what reference service is being provided and how successful the program has been.

A fourth advantage of evaluation is that it helps others learn from a previous program's mistakes, and over the long run will provide support for some general principles which will serve as a basis in the development of new programs.

DISADVANTAGES OF EVALUATION

There are some disadvantages with evaluation which we should not ignore. The most obvious disadvantage is the need for technical skills in the development of an experimental design, and the use of statistics. In this regard librarians must overcome their isolation from colleagues who have the expertise in these areas. We expect faculty to come to the library when they have information problems, We should expect to go to them for answers to our questions about research design and statistics. Therefore librarians should be much more in contact with people in the fields of psychology, sociology, education and statistics, and draw upon their expertise.

Another distinct disadvantage is that research or evaluation is very time consuming. It tends to get in the way of the major responsibility of the reference librarian or a library instruction librarian trying to be at the reference desk so many hours a day or in the classroom talking to students so many hours a week. I would like to re-enforce the suggestion that was made in an editorial in *College Research Libraries* a few months ago that major university libraries should establish an office of research within their library to provide for someone who can do operational research.[1] This kind of resource within the university library would be very helpful to library instruction librarians. I do not think it is possible for individual librarians during their day to day activities to do in-depth research.

They can do some kinds of evaluation, but not most of the sophisticated research that is going to have to occur in the near future if we are to make real progress. This is going to require help from experts in the fields of psychology, sociology, education and statistics, as I formerly mentioned, but it is also going to require people within the library field who have no other responsibility but evaluation of library instruction.

A third disadvantage or difficulty with evaluation is the fact that presently evaluation of library instruction is in its infancy. We have not agreed upon standards for evaluation, or agreed upon methods, or on objectives. We need a good deal more information in order to develop common assumptions about our work. Because we lack these commonalities, it is very difficult to start into a research project.

WHAT IS THERE TO EVALUATE?

If I could outline ideally all the components of a complete evaluation of a bibliographic instruction program, these are the kinds of things I would want to evaluate: First of all, I want to evaluate the students' achievement. Measuring this achievement is somewhat like evaluating proficiency in using a typewriter. You can evaluate whether or not the students know where the keys are, and how a typewriter is put together; you can also evaluate how he uses it; how many mistakes are made and how long it takes to do a given task. We have the same kind of situation in library instruction. You can evaluate the students' knowledge of libraries and library materials which is the *content* of the instruction; you can also evaluate the students' *products,* the result of using the library. We can go one step further and evaluate the *processes* students use to arrive at their product. Therefore our evaluation or research instruments must gather data, on students' knowledge of library arrangement and library reference tools, on the bibliographies students produce as a result of a library search, and on the processes the students use to find the items on their bibliographies. In addition to these cognitive and manipulative skills, the evaluation of bibliographic instruction should look at how the attitudes of students towards libraries and librarians change as a result of that instruction.

We can evaluate the over-all aspects of the program by looking at the management of the program, its position in the library, and the relation of library goals that have been set by the administration for the library. We should not isolate bibliographic instruction from a consideration of the over-all role of the library within the academic institution and how bibliographic instruction contributes to the satisfactory fulfillment of that role. J. Thomas Vogel, in his overview of library evaluation in the *Drexel Library Quarterly* talks about this in considerable detail.[2]   He reminds us that a biblio--graphic instruction program probably means not providing other services. He is asking hard questions of accountability and whether bibliographic instruction is really cost--effective. He is raising the types of questions which administrators are going to ask about reference services and bibliographic instruction.

THE REVIEW OF PAST RESEARCH

I do not intend to examine each research project in depth, but rather will outline some of the strengths and weaknesses in each project. Based on what I have said concerning what there is to be evaluated, I think you will see in these projects that although we have done some evaluation, we have not come anywhere near covering all of the aspects which I have mentioned: the content, the product, the process, the attitudes, and the administrative and economic factors. I will qualify my introduction of this section a little further by saying that I recognize quite clearly that these evaluations as they were originally conceived were not intended to be comprehensive, but I think that as we examine them we can see illustrations of good evaluations and get some ideas of where these evaluations might have gone further.

The Monteith College Library Project[3]

I begin with the Monteith Library Project and separate it from the other projects because I think the Monteith project is old enough now, and has gotten so much attention that we tend to think of the project with a certain kind of awe and reverence, and make the assumption that the things that were learned from that project have been incorporated into what is going on in current bibliographic instruction programs and their evaluation. That simply is not true. The Project is not entirely deserving of the reverence that it is given and the findings of the Project have not been completely included in bibliographic instruction of today. It is very important to recognize that the Monteith Project was a pilot project, and I do not know if everyone is aware of the fact that Patricia Knapp had intended to continue the project for an additional five year period once the general design of the instructional program had been articulated. I am not entirely sure of the reasons why the project was not con--tinued for another five year period, but there were certainly a num--ber of administrative difficulties within Monteith College. There were the awesome problems of coordinating that project with the number of people who were involved, and certainly Patricia Knapp's failing health was an important factor. Be that as it may, it is impor--tant to recognize that this was a pilot program. Knapp was trying to look at the dimensions of the difficulty of integrating bibliographic instruction into the classroom and the curriculum. Furthermore, she was trying to get some idea of how to evaluate the successes and failures of this particular kind of library instruction program. There are no ready answers in the Monteith College Project, only suggested directions for further investigation.

Patricia Knapp, in her discussion of methodology, argues quite convincingly for the use of small samples in the evaluation process rather than long tests and/or questionnaires. Furthermore, she asserts that it would be preferable to use small groups and do intensive evaluation, especially through the use of interview. This is one area that has been used very little in subsequent library instruction evaluation. Patricia used three other instruments for evaluating students' capabilities. First she used performance tests. These tests were administered twice, one more or less immediately following the actual instruction, and a second one a year later. These tests are tasks which demand that a student use a particular reference tool at some specified skill level. The second evaluation was of a bibliographic review which a student prepared as a senior. In doing their senior essay, students were asked to prepare an annotated bibliography on the subject of their paper. That bibliography was then evaluated by a professor, and by a subject specialist. The third form of evaluation was a comparative study by a professor in a non--Monteith college course. Monteith College seniors were taking courses at the University but outside of Monteith College and the professors in those courses were asked to rank their students on the basis of knowledge or familiarity of the literature of the field of courses. The faculty were asked to rank all their students and then the Monteith library personnel looked to see where the Monteith students fell in this ranking.

Despite all of Patricia Knapp's discussion about libraries as complicated bibliographic systems which students should learn about and should function in the library recognizing these systems, she was never able to pull off an evaluation of the process of student use. A quotation from her book[4] indicates her failure to be able to evaluate this process, but then goes on to issue an optimistic outlook for the future. She says,

> When the student had finished all the other tasks, we asked him to prepare a bibliography of not more than twelve items, 'the most important discussions . . . in the sense that they provide what a non–specialist would need to read in order to acquire a reasonably adequate grasp of the topic' on the subject, 'co--operative cataloging.' The topic was one which we could be reasonably certain was not familiar to the student; we knew that the entries in *Library Literature* were not selective enough to provide a good current bibliography. We wanted to see what

kinds of procedures each student would employ when the habitual approaches, through the card catalog and a periodical index, were not fruitful. We hoped that some students might generalize from their experience with Winchell or, at least, that we would be able to discern a logical pattern in their procedures.

The results of the work of our first experimental sample taught us that such expectations were not justified, and we dropped this test from the battery we gave to the second sample. We persist in the belief, however, that the skilled library user should have grasped the concept of the 'structure of the literature' of a subject. He should understand that every field is provided, to a greater or lesser degree, with sources of organized information about terms and concepts, ideas and methods, about people, places, and times, with indexes and abstracts, and with bibliographies, comprehensive and selective, annotated and unannotated, classified and unclassified. And he should be capable of using this knowledge to find his way about in the literature of a subject, even though he is unfamiliar with the field. In other words, we are still convinced that our expectations for this test were disappointed not because the level of library competence it attempted to measure was so high. This level of competence is not just 'picked up' by the bright student. It must be taught.

Knapp is indicating here that the evaluation of the task, or the evaluation of the product, showed some success on the student's part, but because the instruction lacked specific focus on the question of search strategy, they were not able to accomplish that evaluation, and they quickly recognized this and stopped using that evaluation. Therefore, while there has been a lot of talk about Patricia Knapp's concern for instruction of search strategy, we must admit in hindsight that the Monteith Project was not able to achieve that kind of success.

Since no evaluation of the attitudes toward the library or towards librarians was undertaken, we do not learn in the Monteith Project whether students' attitudes toward librarians and libraries were changed by the type of instruction they were given. Students were asked, however, about their attitudes and reactions to the library experiences, course work, and the impact of the library program on their own work. From the questionnaire results, the Project staff attempted to develop a single "response" score. However, they quickly realized that attitudes toward library assignments consist of at least three variables, "understanding the assignment," "seeing value in the assignment," and "enjoying the assignment," which should be studied individually.[5]

6

User Studies

You may wonder why user studies are included in a review of research on bibliographic instruction, but as I indicated in my initial definition of evaluation of library instruction, I think we have to be concerned about the background of students and the kinds of capa-- bilities the students who use our libraries have. We simply have not addressed ourselves to that question in any kind of detail. Informa-- tion scientists and librarians have been studying the literature use habits of scientists for years. However, the number of studies of how undergraduates use libraries and how they get information can prob- ably be counted on one hand and they have all been done fairly recently.

I am not going to try to review all the user studies and what they might tell us about undergraduate use of libraries.[6] What I would like to focus on are what the studies tell us in general about how students use the library and what their attitudes towards the library are. Except for studies of library circulations per student there have been few studies of the nature and dimensions of library use by undergraduates. The most recent study, which contains a good review of the literature, is that of Colleen Amundson.[7] In her study she looks at the information gathering techniques of 311 freshmen in a communications course at the University of Minnesota. The students' assignment was the preparation of a 2500 word report on some topic in which they were interested. Amundson's study is an impressively comprehensive examination of the wide range of problems associated with determining library use by undergraduates. The findings which are most relevant here are:

1. Librarians are the *least* used source of information.
2. Students relied almost exclusively on the *Readers Guide* and the subject headings in the card catalog to locate documents.

These are the sort of conclusions which many librarians, based on their experience, would have expected. But it is nice to have it demonstrated in more concrete terms.

The one major disappointment with her study involves her attempt to explore the hypothesis:[8]

"3. A distinctive pattern of library use will emerge for students with formal training in library usage.

3.1 Students so trained will use libraries more extensively at each stage of their assignment.

3.2 Students trained by librarians will use reference li- brarians more extensively than other students do."

Unfortanately, Amundson does not develop the evaluation of bibliographic instruction component of her study beyond the current state--of--the--art. Her evaluation of student skills and use of the library is based on an objective test which deals only with what I have called above, the content of library instruction. Nowhere in her study does she consider the process of finding information in the library (i.e. was it efficient?) or the quality of the product of a library search (i.e. is there a good bibliography associated with that paper?). However, these were not the main focus of her study and therefore the study should not be overly criticized on that point.

Amundson's study draws a number of other important con--clusions which are useful in considering the background and attitudes of university students and the students' use of libraries. Anyone em-barking on a new program of library instruction should study her thesis for the insight it provides into how students get information for class assignments. While some of her conclusions verify what experienced undergraduate librarians have been saying, she does pro-vide some new insights into the nature of undergraduate information gathering.

What are the attitudes of students toward the library and par-ticularly what are students' perceived attitudes of faculty? John Lubans' studies indicate that we have a real problem on our hands.[9, 10] He concludes from his user surveys that student use of the library is anxiety producing; students enter the library feeling uncomfortable and lacking confidence in their skills. To complicate matters further, the students perceive that instructors assume they all know how to use the library, and the instructors do not give a very high priority to knowing how to use the library. Therefore the student is boxed in by a set of attitudes that he perceives in the faculty and by his own feelings of inadequacy and lack of confidence in using the library. In this situation it is not surprising that Amundson and others find student library use is very minimal and unsophisticated. The user studies indicate that we have a problem not just with the students, but also with faculty. Therefore evalua-tion is an important tool in our discussions with faculty on the importance of bibliographic instruction.

EVALUATION OF INSTRUCTIONAL PROJECTS

There has been no overall evaluation of a bibliographic instruc-tion program for which the data has been published. The closest we can come are two evaluations of specific bibliographic instruction activities. Marvin Wiggins[11, 12] has recently reported on the approach the Reference Staff, in conjunction with the Department of Instructional Research and Development at Brigham Young Uni--versity, have used to develop programmed instruction materials. The first steps have resulted in the production of a guide to the card catalog.[13] I am not so much concerned here with the methods used to develop the instructional materials, although their approach is unique in the field of bibliographic instruction. Rather I wish to emphasize the direct role which objectives played in their work. The

Brigham Young University group found it essential to develop a set of objectives *before* they developed their program. However, the objectives which they have chosen, while behavioral, are not in the context of "real live" library use. Instead, they are written in terms of how a student is to perform in certain objective test situations. Although one test did simulate actual use of the card catalog, no--where in the objectives or the evaluation items are the students evaluated on their effectiveness or efficiency in using the card catalog. And more importantly, there is no evaluation (or objectives) which addresses itself to general questions such as the weakness of the card catalog, or when it is appropriate and inappropriate to use the card catalog.

In a sense, this criticism of the Brigham Young program is unfair since they admit this is only the first step in the development of an instructional program which is presently incomplete. Nevertheless, I think it is important to recognize that while the Brigham Young University approach is a significant improvement, it does not touch on aspects of the product or process of library use which I described above.

One important aspect of evaluation which I believe should have been explored is the attitude of students towards the library and librarians. As I explained above, one of the essential things which an academic bibliographic instruction program must do is overcome some very unfavorable attitudes which students have towards libraries and librarians. I believe it is important, in assessing the success of a program, to know what effects the program had on student attitudes towards the library and librarians.

Hansen[14] and Culkin[15] describe a computer assisted instruction project at the University of Denver library. This project has deliberately simple objectives relating to stimulating the use of reference tools, and orientation to the reference collection, and was not, initially, expected to teach students the use of the library. Certainly the evaluation procedures used, as the investigators noted, will not satisfy everyone. However, the questionnaire they did use elicited a strongly favorable response from the users of the computer terminal. The most unfortunate aspect of the evaluation of the project is the failure to give complete data on the financial cost of such an operation. Complete information is given on actual costs paid for from the library budget, but we are not given total institutional costs for such a project. This kind of data is necessary for responsible administrative decision making.

Comparative studies of different teaching methods and their effectiveness have been a very popular area of educational research. This has been especially true in the development of new methods of instruction (e.g. computers and programmed instruction) and their comparison with traditional forms. In the field of academic library instruction research there have been three thorough studies comparing instructional methods.[16, 17, 18] Each of these studies sets out to compare one instructional method with another (Kuo compares six methods) using the traditional pre–test -- post–test experimental procedure. However, here the similarity ceases. Axeen's program was an undergraduate library science course, while the other two were a part of a course in another subject. Axeen used the Columbia University test[19], which tests only for very basic library skills. From these test results she concluded that the computer approach was more effective than the lecture method. The study however, does not include an evaluation of the process or product of library use and we are thus left without any evidence that the computer taught students to use the library with greater effectiveness and efficiency. Axeen did explore the attitudes of students towards learning by computer (and found no negative attitude), but did not assess whether there were attitude changes towards libraries and librarians.

Kirk, in his study, compared printed programmed instruction and the lecture method. In addition to the pre– and post–test of the content of the instruction, he used evaluation of the bibliographies associated with library papers, and an attitude survey. The results demonstrated that there were *no* significant differences in the effectiveness of the two methods. The use of an evaluation of the bibliographies was an attempt to get at the question of evaluating the product of student use of the library. The method of evaluation differed from that used in the Monteith Library Project in that a librarian did the evaluation using criteria which only indirectly indicated how well the students had done in their search. Unfortunately, the criteria used were somewhat subjective. They have subsequently been refined, and I will discuss them later.

Kuo more recently has suggested that different methods have greater effectiveness. In his study, the six instructional methods have varying degrees of completeness of sensory experience. This range included conventional lecture, audio instruction, slide/audio–tape, television, audiotutorial, and audiotutorial plus a librarian led follow–up.[20] Kuo measured only short term retention of the content of the instruction which we would expect to be greatest in that group with the most sensory experience. In fact, he did find that the audiotutorial group plus the librarian led follow–up was most effective. Kuo did not evaluate actual library use results nor did he examine possible changes in attitude towards the library or librarian.

WHAT NEEDS TO BE DONE? WHERE DO WE GO FROM HERE?

The most important need in library instruction today is to have

objectives. We simply do not have an adequate set of objectives.[21]
The objectives that have been developed for the projects discussed
above all have certain limitations. The most important is that we do
not know the relationship between our enabling objectives[22] and the
general objectives. To be more specific, the card catalog program of
Brigham Young University spends a great deal of time emphasizing
filing rules, the use of the Library of Congress subject heading list,
and the interpretation of the symbols in that subject heading list.
These are mechanical things. Can we demonstrate that knowing
those things enables the student to be a more effective and efficient
user of the library? Should the instruction content emphasize that
kind of thing or are there other things to be emphasized? What we
need is a whole series of explorations of relationships between enabling objectives and general objectives.

Another area that needs exploration is the development of e-
valuation techniques which measure the process and product of library use. All of our evaluations to this point, with few exceptions,
have been related to the content. We ask a student, can you find X
book in the card catalog? Can you identify the parts of an entry in
the *Readers Guide*? Instead we should look at and evaluate the process of student use of the library and the products that result from
the process. But in order to evaluate that use, we need some tools
for evaluation. We are all thoroughly dissatisfied with the kinds of
evaluation tools available. One of the interesting findings of the
Monteith College Project provides a new insight into the Columbia
University Library Orientation Test for Freshmen (the one that has
been around for so many years and has taken the brunt of the
criticism of library tests). Patricia ran a correlation study between
her task performance evaluation and the Columbia test and got a
correlation value which is very high. She concludes, and I think
rightly, that the test, just as the title implies -- a Library Orientation
Test -- is intended to measure the general capabilities of the student.
It cannot be used to test a student's capabilities on a specific task,
and it cannot test sophisticated library use. Yet for some research
projects, it has been used for these purposes, with disastrous results
in terms of the value of the research. Aside from the Columbia test,
there are no recognized standard tests in the library profession that
can be used in testing students' capabilities to use the library. This
is a deplorable situation which has got to change if we are to be able
to interpret results and make some sort of predicitons about the
success or failure of the library instruction programs when they are
implemented in different institutions. I offer for your information
some practical ideas for evaluation of process and product which we
have been using at Earlham. Some of these are not original with us
and I am sorry to say I cannot trace all of their intellectual heritages

back to all those people whom Jim Kennedy, Evan Farber and I have talked to around the country.

The first of these (Appendix B), "Guidelines for keeping a journal on library use," can be very useful in collecting information on how students use the library. Unfortunately, this form of evaluation has some problems if it is to be used in pure research as opposed to use as an instructional feedback mechanism that provides the librarian with general information on how students used the library. The major problem is that the detail with which the journals are kept is very uneven. While some students list every detail, others provide such sketchy results that a qualitative evaluation is impossible. An alternative to this unstructured journal is a series of structured questions that ask students for specific information about their use of certain classes of reference tools and library indexes (Appendix C). While this form standardizes the data collected, it is not entirely appropriate for research since its structure is likely to re-enforce the desired search strategy and by asking certain questions alert students to the essential problems of library searching. In fact, the example in Appendix C has been used at Earlham College as a mechanism for re-enforcing the concepts covered in previous library instruction sessions.

Evaluation of bibliographies which result from student use of the library was used both in the Monteith Project and in Kirk's comparative study. The form used by Kirk, as I mentioned above, was inprecise. Since the completion of that study, the criteria have been revised several times. (The present form is included in Appendix D.) In its present form, there is more precision in each of the criteria statements, therefore communicating to both the student and to other librarians exactly what the person scoring the bibliography was assessing when a score was assigned. The virtue of this set of criteria is that by using it librarians with only modest expertise in the subject area can quickly evaluate the quality of the bibliography. While it certainly will not satisfy someone who assumes that there is an essential list of items on each subject which should appear on any paper on that subject, the criteria do provide an indirect measure of how successful students were in locating material on their topic.

One of the other major needs that we have is to get some evaluation of existing programs. I think it would be a tragedy if we were to go on in library instruction evaluation at this point without getting some evaluation of existing programs. I am thinking particularly of the Model College Libraries grant program of the Council on Library Resources, under which a considerable amount of money has been distributed to fifteen institutions.[23] All of those grants were awarded with the objective of getting the library more involved in the curriculum. It seems to me that almost by definition, that kind of objective requires library instruction, and yet we have very little information from those institutions about the success and failures that they have had. We have a few initial articles on what they are going to try to do and some rosy predictions about the future; and yet although some of those programs are in their fourth of five years, we do not at this point have any kind of evaluation of their success or failures. It will be a waste of considerable sums of money if we do not get evaluation of these projects. I can think of other institutions that have had programs for long periods of time, and it seems to me that if they have been in existence for four and five and ten years, there must be something positive there that keeps them in existence. They are not running on early enthusiasm and early public relations. We ought to be looking at their successes and the limits of that success. We tend to say that if a program has been going for ten years, it must be great. People have said that about our program at Earlham, and yet all of us who participate in that program are un--comfortable by our inability to be certain whether we are being as successful as people say we are, or as we think we are. We need a rigorous, comprehensive evaluation, which would show whether we are being successful or are deluding ourselves.

Finally, we need more user studies. Amundson's and Lubans' studies need to be repeated at other institutions to check for insti--tutional biases and to lend greater weight to their conclusions. We also need studies of faculty attitudes toward student use of the library. If John Lubans' studies on student attitudes, and particu--larly the student's impression of faculty attitudes are correct, then we have a major problem in educating the faculty. I would like to know more about what faculty are really thinking about the role of the use of the library in undergraduate education. It would be help--ful simply to convince faculty that their rhetoric does not match their practice, if that in fact is the situation. I have my hypothesis here that all the discussion about developing independent thinkers and developing people who can educate themselves has a direct cor--ollary in library instruction, and that faculty have not recognized that fact. I would like the evidence to show the faculty what the situation really is.

FOOTNOTES

1 Harris, Michael H. Intuition, research, and the academic library. *College and Research Libraries* 34(4):269 (July, 1973).

2 Vogel, J. Thomas. A Critical Overview of the Evaluation of Library Instruction. *Drexel Library Quarterly* 8(3):315--324 (1972).

3 Knapp, Patricia K. *The Monteith College Library Project.* New York: Scarecrow Press, 1966. 293 pp.

4 *Ibid.,* pp. 68–69.

5 *Ibid.,* p. 76.

6 Two works provide access to the literature: A 1964 bibliography (Richard A. Davis and Catherine A. Bailey, *Bibliography of Use Studies,* Philadelphia, Drexel School of Library Science, 1964, 98 pp.) -- because it is ten years old, has very little on user studies of college students. It is useful for any exploration of user studies, and you can get some idea about techniques for studying user patterns. The second work is *Use, Misuse, and Nonuse of Academic Libraries:* Proceedings of the 1970 New York Library Association College and University Libraries Section Spring meet--ing, which provides some interesting background material on this question.

7 Amundson, Colleen Coghlan. *Relationships Between University Freshmen's Information–Gathering Techniques and Selected Environmental Factors.* PhD Thesis, University of Minnesota, 1971.

8 *Ibid.,* p. 45.

9 Lubans, John. Nonuse of an Academic Library. *College and Research Libraries* 32:362--367 (1971).

10 Lubans, John. Report to the Council on Library Resources as a Fellowship awarded for 1971--72. Mimeographed 1972. (Partially reported in the author's Evaluating Library Uses Education Program, *Drexel Library Quarterly* 8:325–343 [1972]).

11 Wiggins, Marvin E. Use of an Instructional Psychology Model for Development of Library–Use Instructional Programs. *Drexel Library Quarterly* 8:269--279 (1972).

12 Wiggins, Marvin E. The Development of Library Use Instructional Programs. *College and Research Libraries* 33:473--479 (1972).

13 Bradshaw, Charles I. *Using the Library: Card Catalog.* Provo, Utah: Brigham Young University Press, 1971.

14 Hansen, Lois N. Computer–Assisted Instruction in Library Use: An Evaluation. *Drexel Library Quarterly* 8(3):345--355 (1972).

15 Culkin, Patricia B. Computer–Assisted Instruction in Library Use. *Drexel Library Quarterly* 8(3):301--311 (1972).

16 Axeen, Marina E. Teaching the Use of the Library to Undergrad--uates: An Experimental Comparison of Computer--Based Instruction and the Conventional Lecture Method. Urbana, University of

Illinois, 1967 (Available from National Technical Information Service, AD 657 216).

[17]Kirk, Thomas G. A Comparison of Two Methods of Library Instruction for students in Introductory Biology. *College and Research Libraries* 32:465--474 (1971).

[18]Kuo, Frank F. A Comparison of Six Versions of Science Library Instruction. *College and Research Libraries* 34:287--290 (1973).

[19]*A Library Orientation Test for College Freshmen,* Bureau of Publications, Teachers College: Columbia University, 1955. 12 pp.

[20]The paper as published in *College and Research Libraries* is incomplete. The description of the Television Instruction Group (TV) was omitted, and the description of the Audiotutorial Instruction is mislabeled as Television Instruction.

[21]Since this talk was given, the Association of College and Research Libraries' Bibliographic Instruction Task Force has completed a model set of objectives. A copy is included in Appendix A.

[22]Three levels of objectives are used: General Objectives are overall goals of a program; Terminal Objectives break the general objectives down into specific meaningful units; and Enabling Objectives define the specific knowledge or skills which are necessary to achieve the terminal objectives. This terminology comes from the Commission on Instruction Technology's report in *To Improve Learning* (New York, R.R. Bowker, 1970) v. 2, p. 944.

[23]Council on Library Resources. *Annual Report* 14:14, 15:34, 16:12, 17:

APPENDIX A

ACADEMIC BIBLIOGRAPHIC INSTRUCTION: MODEL STATEMENT OF OBJECTIVES

by ACRL Bibliographic Instruction Task Force

While reviewing the model statement a few points should be kept in mind:

1. The model statement's primary purposes are to (a) get academic librarians to focus on and articulate what their instructional objectives should be and to design instructional programs to achieve these objectives, and (b) stimulate research into whether existing programs are achieving these objectives.

2. The objectives are those for an entire program of bibliographic instruction in an academic institution.

3. The objectives are intended to cover bibliographic instruction programs for *undergraduates*. Some objectives are no doubt applicable to any level of student, but these objectives in their totality are intended to speak specifically to the needs of undergraduates.

4. The objectives do not suggest one method of instruction nor should they be used for evaluating a particular instruction unit.

5. An attempt has been made to write the enabling objectives (E's)[1] as *behavoral* objectives.[2] In any institution's revision or individually written objectives the objectives should be specific and measurable.

6. The arrangement of the terminal objectives and the related enabling objectives is not intended to suggest a sequence for an instructional program nor is it intended to suggest an order of significance. The Task Force has debated extensively whether the objectives should include aspects of what have commonly been called orientation in what is supposed to be a statement on bibliographic instruction. While the Task Force is absolutely convinced that orientation is not sufficient neither are we convinced that meaningful instruction can be divorced from orientation to a particular library.

7. The Task Force believes that the primary role of bibliographic instruction is to provide students with the specific skills needed to successfully complete their assignments. But in addition, bibliographic instruction should also serve the more general function of preparing students to make effective life long use of the library regardless of specific course work. Individual librarians or library

staffs must use all of their skills to develop an instruction program that achieves these or revised objectives in the context of the students' course and library use.

The model statement is composed of a series of terminal objectives (T1, T2, T1a, T1b, etc.) written during 1973. These objectives have received the careful attention of the Task Force and other librarians involved in library instruction. Since October 1973, the Task Force has been working on the enabling objectives (E1, E2, etc.) which are listed under each terminal objective. The final version was approved at American Library Association in July, 1974.

OBJECTIVES

General objective:

> A STUDENT, BY THE TIME HE OR SHE COMPLETES A PROGRAM OF UNDERGRADUATE STUDIES, SHOULD BE ABLE TO MAKE EFFICIENT AND EFFECTIVE USE OF THE AVAILABLE LIBRARY RESOURCES AND PERSONNEL IN THE IDENTIFICATION AND PROCUREMENT OF MATERIAL TO MEET AN INFORMATION NEED.

T1. *The student recognizes the library as a primary source of recorded information.*

    E1. Given a list of information needs and services which can best handled by a variety of campus units, the student correctly identifies the library as the best unit for at least 85%* of the appropriate listings. For example, given a list of 25 information needs or services of which 14 are best handled by the library, the student correctly suggests the library for 12 of those 14 items.

T2. *The student recognizes the library staff, particularly the reference staff, as a source of information, and is comfortable seeking assistance from staff members.*

    E1. Given a map of the library the student is able to locate key service points (e.g., circulation, reserve, periodicals). The student can identify the location of information and/ or reference area(s) of the library.

    E2. The student can identify the members of the reference staff by sight and locate their offices.

    E3. (If applicable) the student can identify by name the member(s) of the reference staff best qualified to assist him in his subject major.

    E4. The student asks the reference staff for assistance whenever library–related information is needed.

    E5. When asked about library services the vast majority of students will respond positively to questions such as: "Are there people within the library who are willing to give assistance in locating needed information?" "Do these people give competent assistance?"

T3. *The student is familiar with (or has knowledge of) the library resources that are available to him.*

    a. *The student knows what library units exist on his campus and where they are located. The student knows what major in–*

formation resources and collections are available in these units.

E1. While seeking information from the library, students will use most campus library units which contain substantial material relevant to their topic.

E2. While using the library, students will use a variety of collections within the central library: Documents, pamphlet file, microfilm, etc., as appropriate to their topic.

b. *The student understands the procedures established for using these facilities.*

E1. A student can sign out a library item correctly (as defined by each institution).

E2. The student can interpret library forms (e.g., overdue notices, search forms, hold requests, etc.)

c. *The student knows about the off–campus information facilities available and how to approach their resources.*

E1. A student will ask the reference staff for advice about the possibilities of other information resources outside the "official libraries" of his college or university when those sources do not meet his needs.

E2. A student who has need of materials which the library does not have will request that they be borrowed from another library.

T4. *The student can make effective use of the library resources available to him.*

a. *He knows how to use institutional holdings records (such as the card catalog and serials holdings lists) to locate materials in the library system.*

E1. Given a map of the library the student can correctly identify the location of the library's catalog (e.g., card catalog, book catalog, public shelf list) and other holdings lists in 3* minutes.

E2. The student will correctly identify and explain the purpose of selected elements on a sample catalog entry in 5* minutes. The selected elements will include: the author, title, place of publication, publisher, date of publication, series title*, bibliographic notes, tracings, and call number.

E3. Given a topic or list of topics, the student will accurately list the items found in the catalog on those topics in a specified period of time. The topics will include items which require the student to use the U.S. Library of Congress *Subject headings used in the dictionary catalog of the Library of Congress.* The student will also have to demonstrate his knowledge of form subdivisions, and subject filing rules such as historical subdivisions are filed in chronological order.

E4. Given a list of materials, the student in a specified time, can correctly identify and locate those materials which the library owns. The list shall include incomplete citations, citations which are listed under entries other than the "main entry." It will also include:

Book (individual author)
Book (corporate or institutional author)
Journal (recent issue)
Journal (older or discontinued title)
Newspaper
U.S. Document
Pamphlet
Non--book materials
Microform
Other, as appropriate to the institution

This list will include items which require the student to demonstrate his knowledge of selected filing rules such as: initial articles are ignored in filing, abbreviations are filed as if spelled out, Mc is filed as if spelled Mac, numerals are filed as if spelled out.

b. *He knows how to use reference tools basic to all subject areas.*

E1. Given a map of the library, the student can correctly identify the location of the reference department (and its catalog) in a specified time period.

E2. In a specified time period, the student can identify major reference tools (encyclopedia, dictionary, index) in an unfamiliar field using a guide to the literature such as *Winchell's Guide to Reference Books.*

E3. In a specified time period, the student can list 5 periodical titles (and the indexes which cover them) in an unfamiliar subject field using a directory such as *Ulrich's International Periodical Directory.*

E4. In a specified time period, the student will list five titles available on an unfamiliar topic using a bibliography such as *Subject Guide to Books in Print, Bibliographic Index,* Library of Congress, *Books' Subjects.*

E5. Given a topic with which the sudent is unfamiliar, in a specified time period, he will locate a general introduction to that topic and at least 2 references to further information using an encyclopedia. The topic as stated should require the use of the encyclopedia's index to locate relevant materials.

E6. Given a sample entry, the student will correctly identify selected elements of a typical periodical index entry in a specified period of time. These elements will include:

title of article, title of journal, volume, date, author, pages.

E7. Given a list of topics and a list of indexes (such as *Reader's Guide, SSHI, ASTI, PAIS)* the student will select the index which best covers each topic. At least 85%* of the stu--dents' selections should be correct.

E8. Given the author and title of a book, the student will lo--cate a review of that book in a specified time period using a book review index such as *Book Review Digest,* and *Book Review Index.*

E9. Given a specific topic of current interest, in a specified time period, the student will locate two newspaper articles on that topic using a newspaper index such as the *New York Times Index.*

*E10. Given the name of a witness who has appeared before a Congressional Committee, the student can locate a com-plete citation to that testimony using *CIS Index* in a spec-ified time period.

*E11. Given a topic of recent concern to the federal government, the student can locate citations to information issued by both the Executive and Congressional branches using the *CIS Index* and/or the *Monthly Catalog.*

*E12. Given a specific need for statistical information on the U.S., the student can locate the requested statistics and identify the agency publication from which the statistic was taken using *Statistical Abstract of the United States* in a specified time period.

c. *The student knows how information is organized in his own field of interest and how to use its basic reference tools.*

d. *The student can plan and implement an efficient search strategy using library, campus, and other resources as appropriate.*

e. *The student is able to evaluate materials and select those appro-priate to his needs.*

E1. Given a topic within his major field of interest, in a spec--ified time period, the student will compile a quality bib-liography using an efficient search strategy and keep a diary of his search. A librarian and/or classroom faculty member will judge the quality of the bibliography on the following factors:

    (1) 80% of the entries shall meet one or more of the following criteria:

        (a) be written by recognized authorities in the field.

        (b) be represented in standard bibliographies on the topic.

        (c) appear in a recognized journal in the field.

(2) bibliographic format will conform to accepted standards in that subject field.

A librarian will judge the efficiency of the search strategy as evidenced in the diary. The diary should evidence:

(1) The student clearly defined his topic before or during the initial stages of the search.

(2) The student considered and effectively used alternative search terms throughout his search.

(3) The student consulted an encyclopedia or handbook or other general source to obtain standard data or information on his topic early in his search.

(4) The student searched for and used available bibliographies on his topic.

(5) The student searched relevant indexes, or abstracts to update his information.

(6) The student used the subject card catalog.

(7) The student used bibliographies and/or footnotes in relevant materials found during his search.

(8) The student used book reviews, biographical aids or other sources to help him evaluate materials.

(9) The student made accurate complete bibliographic notes and avoided repeated searches to locate or check citations.

(10) The student located materials of interest to him outside the library.

(11) The student consulted librarians and faculty members for aid and suggestions whenever appropriate.

*An asterisk beside an item or number indicates that the Task Force does not recommend it; it is only suggestive.

FOOTNOTES

1 General objective is the overall goal of the program; terminal objectives break the general objectives down into specific meaningful
units; and enabling objectives define the specific knowledge or
skills which are necessary to achieve the termianl objectives. The
terminology comes from the Commission on Instruction Technology's report in *To Improve Learning* v. 2 (R.R. Bowker, 1970),
page 944.

2 Vargas, Julie S. *Writing Worthwhile Behavioral Objectives.* New
York, Harper and Row, 1972. 176pp.

APPENDIX B

GUIDELINES FOR KEEPING A JOURNAL ON LIBRARY USE

Keeping a journal on your use of various library resources will help to achieve two important goals. The first goal is to improve your bibliographic research skills by gaining insight into your thought processes while doing a literature search for a term paper. The second goal is to inform the reference staff what search strategy and sources you used, in order to suggest strategies and sources which might not have occurred to you.

1. List each source *in the order consulted,* even though *it may not have been helpful.* "Source" should be interpreted as a library bibliographic item used: the card catalog, a dictionary, an index, a reference librarian, an encyclopedia, a bibliography at the end of an article, etc., etc.
2. Under each source listed, describe what you expect to find and what you do find (maybe nothing).
3. If you do find something, note it carefully and then tell why you are going to the next step.
4. Do the same for each step until your bibliography is completed.

Following is an example of a journal entry related to a term paper in education:

My topic is: Teaching English in a bilingual elementary school.
1. The *Encyclopedia of Education.*
2. I expected to find an article that would present an overview of the topic, along with a selective bibliography. I did find two articles, one of which was very helpful and had a good selective bibliography.
3. I followed up the following subject headings in the index:

Bilingual children, teaching of	1:466--472
English in elementary school	3:313, 314, 316
Mexican--Americans, education	6:343--347

I did find a brief but helpful summary of my topic in v. 3, p. 316. This bibliography included one relevant item cited as:

Gaardner, A. Bruce. 1967. "Statement before the Special Sub--committee on Bilingual Education of the Committee on Labor and Public Welfare, U.S. Senate, May 18, 1967." *Florida FL Reporter,* 7, no. 1:33--34, 171. Vol. 1, pp. 468--470 briefly described five approaches to teaching bilingual students. Perhaps I will narrow my topic and focus on just one of these approaches. The bibliography cited about twenty periodical articles, books, parts of books, and government documents. About five of these were on Spanish speaking elementary school students, using the English--as--a--second--language approach.

From this source I went to the card catalog to see whether the library owned the best books on the bibliography.

APPENDIX C

General Biology   Name
Earlham -- Fall -- 1973   Lab Instructor

Library Assignment As Part of the Second Library Exam

In order to get you to focus on your search strategy when using the library, we are requesting that you complete the following form *as you do* your search for the second library exam.* We hope that by doing this you will concentrate not only on the information you are reading, but also on the techniques and procedures you used to find the information and how you proceed from one item (book, period-ical, article, etc.) to another. This sheet is to be handed in at the Science Library (circulation desk) the day you turn in your library exam.

1. I started my library search with: (list the names of the reference tools with which you started your search)

2. Did they lead you to any additional sources of information? Yes. No. If the answer was "yes," list the additional sources,

3. What subject heading(s) did you use in the subject portion of the card catalog? Which had listed under them useful titles?

4. Which review series did you check for material on your topic?

5. List here the 3 or less most significant reviews of your topic which you have thus far identified.

6. What citations did you use in your search of the *Science Citation Index?*

7. What key words did you use in your search of *Biological Ab--stracts*?

8. Did you use any other abstracting or indexing tools? Yes. No. If yes, list which ones.

*A description of library exams is given in Kirk, *College and Research Libraries* 32:465--474 (1971).

APPENDIX D

BIBLIOGRAPHY EVALUATION CRITERIA FOR
UNDERGRADUATE PAPERS IN SCIENCE COURSES

This rating scale has been used irregularly at Earlham College over the last six years to evaluate the bibliographies which accompany library related assignments that science students have completed.

This is not a standard students are trying to achieve but rather suggests the kinds of criteria that should be considered in deciding what are good sources for a science paper. It also reinforces some of the concepts they (the students) have learned about search strategy.

The statements have periodically been revised and, we hope, improved over the last six years. The present form is revised slightly from the one we actually used this past term.

Criteria	*Score*
1. The appropriateness of the material cited as sources of information for a scholarly paper in biology. (Appropriateness = rep--utation of source, age of the source, etc.)	5 4 3 2 1 0
2. The appropriateness of the material cited as sources of information for the particular subject being studied. (Appropriateness = reputation of source, age, author authority)	5 4 3 2 1 0
3. A reasonable number of primary sources, from a variety of titles. This shows some confrontation with the indexing services that are available. (1 point/source)	5 4 3 2 1 0
4. Inclusion of the several most important secondary sources and texts in the field being studied. (2 points/source)	5 4 3 2 1 0
5. Number of references. Anything less than 10 items would raise the question of completeness. This will vary greatly from subject to subject and must be considered a minor point. (Less than 4 sources -- 0 pts.;	3 2 1 0

4–6 sources -- 1 pt.; 7–9 sources – 2 pts.;
10 or more sources -- 3 pts.)

6. Consistent acceptable format used in the   3 2 1 0
cited literature section. (Inconsistent for--
mat, incomplete information – 0 pts.; in–
consistent format, complete information –
1 pts.; unacceptable consistent format,
complete information -- 2 pts.; acceptable,
consistent format with complete informa--
tion -- 3 pts.)

LIBRARY INSTRUCTION: THE MYTHOLOGY
OF EVALUATION

Richard R. Johnson
Program Manager
Exxon Education Foundation

The change in the title of this paper came about through a typographical error. On one draft the "od" of methodology was left out and another individual reading the title called to ask me if that syllable should be added or the "e" should be changed to "y." On reflection the latter course seemed more appropriate: Webster's *Third International Dictionary* defines "myth" as: "a story that is usually of unkown origin and at least partially traditional, . . . usually of such character as to serve to explain some practice, belief, institution or natural phenomenon." Perhaps the only way in which the material that follows departs from that definition is in lacking a coherent narrative to cover the beliefs and rituals which have grown up in the field of evaluation and the design of research. What follows here is an attempt in part to pass on to you some of that myth, and in part, while debunking its ritual use, to show its utility.

While it may be quite presumptuous to say so in the midst of the present gathering, I must confess that I have often suspected that library classification systems, whether Dewey Decimal or Library of Congress, were not handed down to us on tablets of stone. Since I am an outsider in this field I cannot claim that this suspicion about classification schemes should be taken seriously; however, I can report to you as an experimental psychologist, that the ten command-ments of evaluation design do not have such a transcendental origin. Although there are many books of holy writ on the design of educa-tional evaluations, these represent, at best, idealized descriptions of past practice or norms developed by the practicing community. Abraham Kaplan in *The Conduct of Inquiry* points out the distinc-tion between the process an evaluator is going through in doing re-search, and the reconstructions we make of the process in books on research and evaluation:

> "Scientists and Philosophers use a logic -- they have a cog-nitive style which is more or less logical -- and some of them also formulate it explicitly. I call the former *logic-in--use*, and the latter the *reconstructed logic.* We can no more take them to be identical or even assume an exact

correspondence between them, than we can in the case of the decline of Rome and Gibbon's account of it, a patient's fever and his physician's explanation of it."[1]

Our discussion today of the logic of evaluation for library instruction is therefore necessarily a reconstructed logic and as a prescription for practice. I can offer you no magic recipe to follow, no algorithm to learn, no ritual to perform which will insure that your instructional program will be automatically, adequately evaluated.

Perhaps it would be better for us to conceptualize our interaction this afternoon as paralleling that between a house builder and an architect: there are individuals who can build a house without plans and end up with a structure that meets their goals quite well. By the same token I am sure there are individuals who are able to evaluate educational programs without tutelage from so-called experts in the design of evaluation. On the other hand, as the structure of questions becomes more complex and as the goals of the evaluation become more sophisticated, it may be useful to have a blueprint to guide the evaluation so that we can at least identify where structural defects could occur and plan accordingly. I come to you then, not offering a comprehensive blueprint to cover any evaluation of library construction, but rather pointing to the characteristics of blueprints which you might adopt in putting together your own plans of evaluation.

The major thesis of my remarks today will be that any attempt to evaluate library instruction needs to be carefully considered and planned out *before* a modification in instruction is attempted. Certainly attempts can be made to evaluate an instructional program which is already underway, but under such circumstances many options for conducting the evaluation are foreclosed. In addition, the attempt to plan ahead for evaluation of an instructional sequence may very well clarify and improve the program itself. I suspect that the greatest benefit which may come out of the recent hue and cry for "competency-based" education and "behavioral objectives" will come from the pressure on an individual to plan ahead, considering not just the sequence of topics he wishes to cover, or how he will fill the instructional time, but rather what kinds of changes he plans to facilitate in students by his instruction. When you have considered the ways in which you might demonstrate by your evaluation how a student does something differently in the library as a function of your instructional program, you may be well on your way toward redesigning that program.

The Influence of Purpose on Process

One of the first questions to be asked in pre-planning an evaluation effort concerns the purpose of the evaluation. Is the evalua-

32

tion a "formative" effort designed to guide the further development of the instructional program or is it a "summative" evaluation designed to reach some final conclusion about the validity of the program? The effort and amount of money that will be spent in each of the two cases probably will differ significantly and the design of the evaluation should probably vary as well. If you have just designed a brief instruction program to be given during freshman orientation week and one of the main questions that you have concerns whether you have included the right kinds of topics, then a brief questionnaire designed to elicit information from these same students as they are carrying on course work later in the year, or an examination of course materials to ascertain the kinds of library materials the students use most often may be appropriate. On the other hand, after such an instructional program has been developed, it may be useful to provide for a far more stringent evaluation to determine whether library resources should continue to be expended upon this kind of activity or diverted to some other function.

Besides determining the appropriate questions to be asked, you need also to consider for whom the answers are intended. An evaluation effort to satisfy yourself and your staff that you are on the right track or have produced an effective educational sequence requires a far different plan than one which is designed to satisfy an outside funding agency or indicate to a dean or the college community the viability and utility of a portion of the library program. Under the latter conditions you need to consider in addition what kinds of questions these individuals would ask and the kinds of answers which would most adequately deal with these questions within a reasonable expenditure of resources.

In any case, the first step in designing evaluation should involve laying out the various questions which could be asked, assigning priorities to getting particular answers and considering the resources available which may be usefully spent in the process.

Measurement of Outcomes

A major concern in any measurement which focuses on providing answers to questions about an instructional program has to do with what counts as an adequate answer. When you have completed an instructional sequence with a group of students, you may be content with a warm glow and a gut feeling that the students enjoyed it and learned a great deal. However, even when the evaluation answers are only for your own use, it is a good idea to check up on yourself. I can recall during my earlier years of teaching that one of the class sessions I had videotaped, represented to me what I thought was a particularly lively discussion. On later viewing the videotape, I discovered that only about two--thirds of the students had actively taken part and that while some of them had spoken up a number of times, I had still monopolized and manipulated the discussion.

Even under the most informal evaluation conditions, you can still train yourself to note precisely how many students ask ques-- tions, roughly what percentage of time was spent in note taking by the class, and how many students stayed after the instructional session or came back at a later time to talk to you further about the material. In addition, by monitoring the content of the questions and comments during a class period, you should be able to tell whether at least some of the class is understanding the material and following your exposition. Sampling errors are particularly signifi- cant in more informal modes of evaluation. That student who stayed after class to tell you how much he got from your presentation may not be a true representative of the class. By the same token, that especially keen question injected in the discussion may not really represent the level of interest or comprehension for the entire group. Only be checking on these impressions and by paying particular attention to the *range* of student responses and reactions can you hope to have a balanced view of the outcomes of an instructional sequence.

In situations where the answers to our questions about an in-- structional program are meant to satisfy others as well as ourselves, the requirement for inter--subjectivity* or even verifiability of our evidence becomes necessary. It is under these conditions that our attempts to measure focus more heavily upon a third party in the evaluation process. The third party may be represented by the stu-- dents, testifying to their experience of the instruction, or another individual who has had some chance to observe the instruction or its effects independently. In addition, any physical residues left by the course, such as papers or bibliographies developed by the students, records of their library use or achievement in related courses may also fill this function.

Typically when one thinks of evaluating any instructional se-- quence, the most usual measurement considered is a questionnaire given to the students who have participated. There is nothing wrong with this kind of information if it answers the kinds of questions raised in the evaluation process: indeed, it is relatively easy informa-- tion to collect and collate. The major problem, however, with this type of questionnaire data is that it is often too easily set up as *the* evaluative technique without consideration given for the goals of the

---

*A term used by Kaplan in *The Conduct of Inquiry* to indicate the necessary communication of trans--individual understanding of e-- vents in order to move beyond pure subjectivity.

evaluation. In addition, the design and interpretation of such ques--tionnaires may be treated far too casually. For example, many people collecting classroom evaluation on faculty members apparent--ly do not realize that student responses to such questionnaires are typically skewed in the positive direction. Thus, if the respondents' tendencies in answering such questionnaires are to emphasize the positive, it is important for anyone examining these data to recognize this and adjust the interpretation accordingly. Similarly, studies have shown that people answering questionnaires tend to agree with positive statements at a much greater rate than they disagree with their opposites. This tendency to assent needs also to be taken into account in both designing a questionnaire and interpreting the results. Unless the questionnaire is quite long, it is probably not a good idea to use questions which elicit true–false or yes--no answers. A great deal more information can be obtained by using 3, 5, or 7 point scales allowing a range of responses between agreement and disagreement. Under these conditions you should be able, both to learn more and to have more reliable answers.

Questionnaires can vary in their individual items as to the level of generality (e.g., "Did you like this course?" vs. "Was this instruc--tor stimulating in his presentation?") as well as focusing on issues ranging from actual reports to attitudes and impressions. Well--de-signed questionnaires on library instruction instead of asking, "Was this instruction useful?" might develop a number of more specific questions some of which ask for factual reports such as, "How many times did you use *Biological Abstracts* during the last term?".

In addition to the simple questionnaire given to students during the last instructional session, there are a number of other modifica--tions for eliciting different types of information from students. The instructed groups could be sampled over time with the same ques--tionnaire to determine the time order of effects of the instruction. Questionnaires may begin with general open–ended questions to elicit relatively non–directed responses and then subsequently probe specific questions seeking directed answers which the instructor wants to follow.

In addition to the more typical written instrument used to elicit student comments, a number of other techniques are available to get direct evaluation information from the student. A sampling of the instructional group can provide several individuals who may be in-terviewed in depth by an outside party pursuing particular questions. Perhaps an even more ingenious elicitation of direct comments from students involves getting a small group of students together to talk to a tape recorder about the course of instruction they have received. If the students are presented with written questions that the in--structor would like to have them deal with in the course of their discussion, this kind of exercise can be properly focused. One advantage of this group process is the condensation of data provided the instructor (he is not listening to or reading extended comments of many students). However, even more significant than this, the students in commenting upon the instructional program interact with each other. The gripes of an individual student will be modified by the reactions of other students to his statements. By the same token, one student may be stimulated into commenting upon a particular aspect of the instruction which he might have forgotten to mention if he had been either writing or speaking by himself.

In addition to the direct request to the student to supply information in evaluating a course of instruction, there are a variety of other kinds of data which are useful for evaluation. To the extent that the outcomes of the instruction have been defined in relation to certain kinds of knowledge or skills that the student should develop during the course of instruction, direct tests on these accomplishments are possible. Such tests may be used as a regular part of the instructional program or may be developed in conjunction with other college courses which the student is taking in parallel or will take subsequently. To the extent that it is not feasible to assay these accomplishments directly by developing instruments for that purpose, it may be possible to monitor student papers and other tasks which involve the use of this knowledge or these skills.

Finally, it is also possible to monitor changes in a student's use of the library either directly by monitoring the activities of a subgroup of the students, or by examining archival data available from the records of the library. In the former case, for example, a group of students may be enlisted to keep a log of their use of the library including time allocated to various kinds of activities and the sequence of sources consulted in retrieving information. In the latter case, records on books taken from the library, use of reserve books, requests for inter--library loan, etc., may be consulted. To the extent that these kinds of data prove useful in evaluating a variety of aspects of the library's program, it may be worth considering the kinds of information collected on various forms and the type of record keeping maintained in relation to regular library transactions. If there are useful data here, and if they can be retrieved readily, then slight increases in the time spent or cost of developing these data may be insignificant in relation to the payoff.

Some of the kinds of data mentioned above may be relatively expensive to collect. In relation to any evaluation question asked it is important to consider the kinds of information that are needed and the importance attached to getting certain kinds of answers in relation to their cost. In many cases a compromise can be made by using sampling techniques to obtain the data. If it is not feasible to test an entire group of students who have received library instruc-- tion, then a subset of these students may be asked to come in to take a test demonstrating skills acquired, or to keep logs of their use of the library or turn in papers from other classes which involved in some way library work. By the same token, if it is impractical for the library staff to develop certain kinds of records on a regular basis, then a sampling may be made over set periods of time to get an estimate of the data that might be available if there were continuous record keeping. For example, it might be useful for the reference librarians to keep records, occasionally, on the students who come to them for help and the kinds of requests they get. If nothing else, these records might suggest some of the kinds of educational pro-- grams that need to be developed by the library.

While using sampling techniques may be an excellent way to cut down the work required in collected evaluative data, it is important to recognize the dangers inherent in this approach to evaluation. Any sampled subset whether of students or of occasions, ought to represent the larger portion of which it is assumed to be a sample. Thus, if you choose students from an instructed group, it is crucial that this be done randomly to insure that the variability within the group be represented. While one can attempt to represent known subgroups within a group (e.g., males versus females or upper class versus lower class students), the sampling within these subclasses should still be random. The reason for this is two--fold: (1) By random sampling, you have insured that you as the investigator have not selected particular cases, whether consciously or unconsciously to bias the outcomes. Thus, random sampling is a guarantee to an outside observer that the data collected were not biased in their sampling by you. (2) All techniques of statistical inference are based upon probability distributions which call for random sampling to estimate population parameters. To the extent that random pro- cedures are not used, the estimates of these population parameters cannot be determined within known levels of confidence.

Perhaps the most important point which can be reiterated con- cerning the kinds of data to be collected in any evaluation of library instruction is that one ought to consider first the kinds of questions that are being asked and then determine the appropriate way to answer these. There are many different kinds of data which could be collected, each type having its own peculiar advantages and disad-- vantages. An even stronger case for a particular conclusion from the evaluation can be made if several different kinds of data are collected concurrently with all pointing toward the same outcome. An ex- cellent reference which explores a number of very imaginative types of data for collection in social science research is *Unobtrusive Mea- sures: Non--reactive Research in the Social Sciences* by Webb,

Campbell, Schwartz and Sechrest.[2]

Problems in Evaluating Educational Programs
After you have considered carefully the kinds of questions that you want to ask and the types of data that will provide the best answers to these questions, there are still some significant problems in developing an evaluation program. While the following do not ex--haust the list of possibilities, they do represent some of the major pitfalls in this area of evaluation. A more complete examination of some of these as well as additional problem areas in the design of research can be found in books on experimental design for social science research.[3, 4, 5] The so--called "Hawthorne" effect may occur when any individual or group is given special treatment. Under these conditions the behavior of the group may change, not only as a result of the particular effects of the treatment, but also because of the fact that the group has been singled out and handled in some different way. Thus, if you give one subgroup of the fresh--man class library instruction while not providing it to other students of the class, this could lead to changes in student behaviors that are not specific to the particular instructional techniques or content provided. The fact that these students may later use the library more than other freshmen does not prove that the particular presen--tation was efficacious: instead it could be that a general discussion over tea with the members of the library staff could have produced the same result, greater interest in the library. It is important, in considering the evaluation of any instructional program, to deter--mine precisely what aspects of the program are being evaluated and to set up some means by which the effectiveness of these may be determined.

Every measurement involves comparison. In noting that a par--ticular student uses three types of reference materials to develop a bibliography of seventeen items, there is in addition to this report of fact a comparison with other events that might have been. The com--parison could involve a successive comparison with this student's previous behavior before library instruction, or a simultaneous com--parison with other students of similar background who have not had the library instruction, or a comparison against some absolute stan--dard (i.e., there are x types of reference materials which could have been used to develop a bibliography in this field). In designing an evaluation, it is important for you to recognize which kinds of com--parison are appropriate to consider in answering the questions posed about the instructional program. The best strategy in evaluating an instructional program is to make the comparison explicit and then do everything possible to insure that only the aspect of the instructional program being evaluated varies between the comparison groups or occasions. If you are evaluating the method by which you are presenting a particular kind of information to students, then another group of students should have a chance to acquire this same infor-- mation in a different way. If you are evaluating the efficacy of a par-- ticular excercise in getting students to develop a certain skill, then you ought to compare this with the way in which the skill is devel- oped by another group of similarly motivated students. While in the beginning stages of developing an instructional program for your library, you might have asked questions concerning whether any type of library instruction was better than none at all, at later stages of your evaluation, you will certainly want to fine tune it to focus more specifically on particular issues. To this end, you should be sure to make the comparisons involved in your evaluation explicit and set up appropriate groups to rule out problems of confounded variables and a "Hawthorne" effect.

Any measurement performed on human beings risks inducing the "guinea pig" effect. If you begin asking students how many books they take out in a week, you may find that students when asked this question regularly begin taking out more books. Re-- actions of "subjects" to being measured may be either positive, with the subject trying to help out, or may be negative if the student resents being measured and reacts negatively to the program for which the measurement is only a part. There are three ways by which you can deal with the reactivity of students to being meas- ured: (1) You can do everything you can to hide the measurement device and/or the purpose of the measurement. This can range all the way from covert observation of students using the library to placing items evaluating library instruction within a more general course evaluation questionnaire to using tests or papers apparently designed to evaluate learning of course content, but actually check-- ing on the development and use of library resources. Obviously, such techniques of reducing reactivity demand careful ethical considera- tion concerning the informed consent of the individuals being meas-- ured. (2) You can apply the measurements over a period of time so that much of the reactivity to being measured habituates and dis-- appears. A student asked to keep a log upon how he uses the library may initially react by spending more time there and taking out more books. However, as the logging period continues, it is likely that the initial reactions to the observation will disappear. (3) You can at- tempt to gather data which are unlikely to have been influenced by reactivity. The records of book withdrawals or requests for inter- library loan mentioned above are unlikely to have been influenced by the "guinea pig" effect. The book by Webb, Campbell, Schwartz and Sechrest, mentioned above, is an excellent source for a variety of non-reactive techniques.

The "Pygmalion" or "Rosenthal" effect[6] refers to the finding that an individual having preconceptions about the outcome of a particular research project is likely to influence the data developed, even though unconsciously. Studies in this area seem to suggest that the influence comes via selection and interpretation of the data and/ or direct influence on the responses of subjects. While at first glance this appears to be a relatively esoteric research problem, it is important to stress the fact that you, as a believer in the instructional program you have developed, may not be the best person to be involved in the evaluation of that program. If the evaluation process involves face--to--face communication with students who have been through the program, there is a strong possibility that the structure of the interview and your later interpretation of it could lead to unconscious bias in the data. By the same token, if you are reading research papers produced by students who have been involved in your instructional program as well as papers by a control group, your interpretation of which represent the more sophisticated use of the library could be influenced by knowledge of which papers come from each of the groups. It is for these reasons that much of the scoring and interpretation of data in more sophisticated experiments is typically turned over to third parties and even then as much scoring as possible is done blind, i.e., without knowledge of which group of individuals is represented by a particular set of papers. While it may not be feasible to bring in another individual to be involved in your evaluation if the questions being asked are mainly for your information, in any effort aimed at producing more sophisticated information for outside agencies, attempts should be made to insure the objectivity of the data and to separate the particular outcomes of the evaluation from the biases of the person running the instructional program.

The study of the methodology of evaluation by undergraduate students often leads many to the conclusion that doing good research is impossible. After cataloging all the pitfalls (and I haven't mentioned all of them here) and recognizing all the limitations on conclusions, one may feel that no study can make a definitive statement. However, if one continues to consider the evaluation effort as merely an attempt to ask questions and design the best possible answers in relation to the action required, then it becomes apparent that an individual design for evaluation does not have to be perfect. Rather, it needs to return significantly better information for making a decision than would be available through guess and gut feeling. The push toward improving that "significantly better" information can be refined as much as time and financial resources will permit. A college in deciding upon which student to admit for its program of study cannot spend infinite resources to examine all possible records on an individual. Rather, it decides upon the amounts of time and money it can invest in types of information that have the greatest leverage on making that decision with the highest possible "batting average." In the same way, in considering the instructional programs we prepare for these students, we need to expend the appropriate resources to select and adjust techniques which will have as good a "batting average" in terms of instructional outcomes.

REFERENCES

1. Kaplan, Abraham. *The Conduct of Inquiry.* San Francisco: Chandler, 1964.

2. Webb, Eugene J., and others. *Unobtrusive Measures: Non-reactive Research in the Social Sciences.* Chicago: Rand Mc-Nally, 1966.

3. Campbell, D.T., and Stanley, J.C. *Experimental and Quasi-experimental Designs for Research.* Chicago: Rand McNally, 1966.

4. Cage, N.L. (ed.). *Handbook of Research on Teaching.* Chicago: Rand McNally, 1963.

5. Kerlinger, F.N. *Foundations of Behavioral Research.* New York: Holt Rhinehart and Winston, 1964.

6. Rosenthal, R., and Rosnow, R.L. (eds.). *Artifact in Behavioral Research.* New York: Academic Press, 1969.

EVALUATION OF COMPUTER–ASSISTED LIBRARY
USE INSTRUCTION

Patricia Culkin, Operations Research Librarian
University of Denver Libraries

The evaluation of the University of Denver's Computer–Assisted Library Use Instruction Program[1] was planned in two phases, each phase relating sequentially to specific objectives. These objectives were:
1. to advertise existence of basic reference materials
2. to offer an alternative to the traditional reference interview to beginning researchers
3. to offer systematic instruction in the use of basic reference materials.

Because of the substantive difference in the nature of these object–ives – the first two relate to the viability of the medium, the third to the curriculum offered via that medium -- it was felt that the evaluation methodology had to be structured in such a way as to allow the medium to become established before the curriculum itself was fully tested.

Consequently, the first phase of the evaluation was simple and uncomplicated, designed to allow users an opportunity to become accustomed to CAI as an alternative method of library instruction while at the same time testing its advertising capability and its potential for acceptance among university library users. Would CAI be capable of increasing awareness of basic reference materials and would university library users, given their particular self--concept, be amenable to being taught basic library skills by machine? Statistical analysis of certain types of correlative data was eventually chosen as the technique most likely to provide valid answers to these questions. Results of these statistical analyses are presented in the next few pages.

The following chart indicates the correlation between number of reference desk contacts and number of CAI contacts during a series of eight academic quarters. The reference figures include per--sonal contacts of both an informational and directional nature, but do not include telephone calls. The number of CAI contacts was furnished from a computer accounting.

	Reference	CAI	Total	% CAI
Fall Quarter 1970	4991	–	4991	–
Winter Quarter 1971	4676	--	4676	--
Spring Quarter 1971	4234	--	4234	–
Summer Quarter 1971	3927	--	3927	--
Fall Quarter 1971	5362	600	5962	10.1
*Winter Quarter 1972	4874	825	5699	14.5
Spring Quarter 1972	4325	795	5120	15.5
Summer Quarter 1972	3720	510	4320	12.1
**Fall Quarter 1972	15304	1716	17020	10.1
Winter Quarter 1973	12990	1520	14510	10.5
Spring Quarter 1973	10200	1234	11434	10.8
Summer Quarter 1973	5998	994	6992	14.2
Fall Quarter 1973	15136	1682	16818	10.0
TOTAL (exludes 1970/71)	77909	9876	87785	11.3 av-- erage

*First *full* academic quarter for which CAI statistics are available.
**First quarter after relocation to new building. CAI terminal feat--
ured much more prominently in main lobby.

The figures above indicating that CAI has consistently accounted for at least 10% of total reference contacts have been considered
sufficient to demonstrate that CAI is capable of making a significant
contribution to the advertisement of reference materials. Reference
contact statistics for a period of four academic quarters preceding
installation of CAI were included to demonstrate that CAI increased
total number of contacts rather than reducing reference load. The
large jump in total contacts beginning Fall 1972 is attributable to the
fact that the main library and its branches were consolidated into a
new, attractive and accessible building in the interim preceding that
quarter.

Cost figures for the CAI service are based on the per contact
totals charted above. CAI is available as many hours per day as the
library is open. During academic quarters, this amounts to 16 hours
per day weekdays, 8 hours Saturday, 11 hours Sunday – a total of
100 hours per week. Interim periods between quarters account for
another 45 hours per week, with the total approximating 5000 hours
of operation annually. Figuring service hours against annual equip--
ment lease costs[2] indicates that the CAI service costs $.25 *per hour*
to operate.

$1236 divided by 5000 hrs./year = .2472   or $.25 per hour
A similar comparison between total annual number of contacts for
the 1972/73 academic year against lease costs for that year indicates

that the *per contact* CAI cost is $.23.

$1236 divided by 5465 1972/73 CAI contacts = .2262

or $.23 per CAI contact

When the percentage of the reference salary budget indicating hours of scheduled desk time is compared to total annual number of desk contacts, the figure is in the area of $.70 per contact.

$74,265 Reference salary budget, 1972/73

x   .42 % scheduled desk time =

$31,191 salaried desk time

$31,191 divided by 44,492 ref. contacts 1972/73 = .7010

or $.70 per ref. contact

Of course, the variance in the per contact cost cannot be considered too significant until data is gathered comparing the effectiveness of reference librarians versus computers as instructors, but the $.23 per contact cost has been considered low enough to justify contin-- uance of the program through the curriculum evaluation stage.

The second objective, offering an alternative to the traditional reference interview, was tested via an optional point--of--use quest-- ionnaire (copy appended). Again, this method was chosen as being the most efficient method of determining subjective reaction, while at the same time being the least likely to interfere with the user's machine experience. The relatively simple questionnaire consists of nine questions, and is based loosely on a questionnaire used to eval-- uate a portion of Project Intrex at Massachusetts Institute of Tech-- nology. The first two questions solicit accounting information to supplement computer records and the last seven solicit users' initial reaction to machine instruction. Users are asked to complete ques-- tionnaires during the last segment of each CAI unit and also by a small, typewritten message taped to the terminal. 2163 question-- naires have been collected over the eight--quarter testing period and these 2163 respondents have accounted for a total of 3028 units. By comparing number of contacts experienced by respondents with total number of contacts, we have estimated a 31% response rate to the questionnaire.[3]

3028 units divided by 9876 contacts = .3066   or   31%

The first question provides information about the user's edu-- cational level.

1. What is your status with the University?

Undergrad. *1014*   Grad. *635*   Faculty *60*

Staff *55* Special *399*   TOTAL: *2163*

This data gives us an indication as to distribution by level of CAI users. It breaks down as follows:

Undergraduates   ---46.8%

Graduates   ---29.4%

Faculty   --- 2.8%

45

Staff   — 2.5%
Special (visitors,
      etc.)   ---18.4%

Question two gives us data concerning the relative popularity of the different curriculum units, and this information combined with specific comments gathered through questions 7–9 have led to some modification of the curriculum. The distribution of respondents by curriculum units is as follows:

	Number of Respondents	% of respon.
How to Find Biographies:		
Living Persons	134	6.2
Deceased Persons	85	3.9
Authors	98	4.5
How to Find Book Reviews:		
General Books	106	4.9
New Books, within last 3 months	90	4.2
Old Books, before 1905	35	1.6
How to Use the Card Catalog:		
Author--Title catalog	385	17.8
Subject catalog	221	10.2
How to Use General Information Sources:		
Encyclopedias	152	7.0
Almanacs, Yearbooks, Statistical Sources	130	6.0
How to Use Periodical Indexes:		
Readers Guide	332	15.3
Social Science and Hu-- manities Index	221	10.2
PAIS Bulletin	111	5.1
How to Use Abstracts:		
General comparison of Ab- stracts and Indexes	125	5.8
Biological Abstracts	130	6.0
Dissertation Abstracts	107	4.9
Psychological Abstracts	86	4.0
ERIC Education Information System:		
Research in Education (RIE)	159	7.4
Current Index to Journals in Education (CIJE)	91	4.2

Term Paper Research Techniques:
Search strategy   230   10.6
TOTAL   3028   10.6

The above figures indicate that the units on more simple per--
iodical indexes and on the card catalog are the most popular, ac--
counting for 58.6% of the total units taken. Correlation of the data
from questions one and two, however, indicates that the majority of
respondents taking easier courses are undergraduates, while the ma--
jority of users selecting more difficult units (e.g. *Dissertation Abstracts, Psychological Abstracts, Biological Abstracts, ERIC,* etc.) are
at the graduate level. This correlation has served to discount to some
extent the curiosity factor that we anticipated. It indicates in a
general way that users are selecting courses which relate directly to
their library use instruction needs.

Questions three through six solicit direct and subjective re--
sponse to machine instruction. The questionnaire was designed so
that a positive answer to these questions could be construed as
positive reaction to machine learning, and a negative response con--
strued as negative reaction. The following percentages of positive
response have indicated to our satisfaction that library instruction via
computer is acceptable to University of Denver library users.

	Total Respondents	*% Positive*
3. Do you feel that you learned something from these courses that you didn't know before about the use of library tools? yes *1759* no *404*	2163	81
4. Do you prefer this method of instruction to asking a librarian? yes *1620* no *543*	2163	75
5. Do you prefer it to the do--it--yourself method? yes *1844* no *319*	2163	85
6. Do you plan on taking any more courses? yes *1791* no *372*	2163	83

The potential for acceptance of CAI by university library users
indicated by this positive response was corroborated by answers to
questions seven through nine. These tabulations are presented be--
low.

7. If (you do not plan on taking
   any more courses), why not?
   a. The courses were too com--
   plicated. *163*
   b. The courses were not com--
   plicated enough. *492*
   c. The courses were not re--
   lated to my library needs.
   112
   d. The CRT terminal was too
   difficult to use. *62*
   e. Other. *127*   956   44.2
8. Would you like to see more and
   different kinds of courses being
   offered? yes *1621* no *211*   1832   11.5
9. Do you have any comments to
   make about this type of in--
   struction in general? *413*   413   -----

Question seven was devised specifically to solicit negative responses, yet as the results indicate, only 44.2% of the respondents bothered to answer it at all. This was the *only* question that has less than a 84% response rate, except for question nine which solicited specific comments. Furthermore, even though 44.2% found fault with some aspect of the program, only 11.5% of those answering question eight were unwilling to see more and different kinds of courses being offered. Many useful extensions of the CAI concept were suggested in the comments written in response to question nine.

Thus, even though some respondents found fault with the curriculum, they were amenable, and in some cases most anxious, to continue experiments with it. On the basis of these tabulations and the general interest in library CAI that the questionnaire response seems to indicate, the decision has been made to continue the project through a strict curriculum evaluation stage.

This curriculum evaluation, the subject of phase two of the evaluation process, is scheduled to be implemented in September 1974. The current intention is to create a test group of CAI users through the names and addresses furnished on the questionnaires, determine their educational level and general library sophistication, and then test them against similar groups receiving other types of library instruction. These other groups will include students in a two-credit course on undergraduate library research taught by the Reference Department, students in selected library research courses taught by various graduate programs, and selected outreach groups contacted on a one--shot basis. They will also be tested against a specifically selected group which has received no library instruction. A workbook is being prepared for use as a text in the undergraduate library research course, and segments of this workbook will correlate very closely to segments of the CAI curriculum. These segments will be adapted for teaching and evaluation of performance of all the test groups.

Results of this curriculum evaluation will hopefully be as positive as the response to the medium itself, but if the results are not encouraging, the committment to the concept of library CAI will be continued through several stages of curriculum modification. The ultimate advantage of CAI is that the curriculum is infinitely manipulable, and given the significance of the concept of individualized instruction, we feel an obligation to continue the program until the possibilities for modification have been exhausted. Preliminary results from this stage of the evaluation should be available early in 1975.

REFERENCES

1 For a detailed description of this program see the author's Com--puter--Assisted Instruction in Library Use, *Drexel Library Quar--terly* 8:301–311 (July, 1972).

2 Computer time costs are not allocated back to the service, but are absorbed by a university research fund.

3 Computer records do not distinguish between users so it is im--possible to compare the number of respondents with the total number of users. We have, instead, compared the number of *units* taken by respondents, as indicated on the questionnaire, to total number of units taken altogether, as furnished by the computer accounting, to estimate total response rate to the questionnaire.

EVALUATING THE AIMLO PROJECT

Betty Hacker, Assistant Reference Librarian
and
Richard Stevens, Reference Librarian
Colorado State University

In order to set the stage for a description of our efforts to evaluate the AIMLO* project, let me tell you rather briefly about the background of its development. Library instruction at Colorado State University has followed the traditional pattern of freshman English class lectures and tours of the library. However, an ever-rising enrollment led to increased demands on the time of the reference staff for tours and lectures. There were more frequent disruptions for patrons using the library as English classes trudged, sometimes unwillingly, through the building. When the university installed a cable television system, the reference department decided to utilize this new medium. We produced a videotape lecture to provide library instruction as well as a film tour of our then new library building. Videotape permitted the English department to bring library instruction to the students in their classrooms at times convenient to the instructor. It also freed the reference staff from repetitive and time–consuming library tours and lectures. The evaluation of our videotape presentation revealed that students learned at least as much from it as they did from "live" lectures by librarians.

A few years ago, when our English department dropped its term paper research class, in which videotape had been used and in which most freshmen had been enrolled, we lost our audience. Because there seemed to be no other course into which our library instruction videotape could be fitted, and because we anticipated a consequent increase in the amount of repetitive instruction on a one–to–one basis at the reference desk, we set out to explore the possibilities of a new approach to basic library instruction. It would be designed to provide information to a student at the *time* when he needed it and at the *point* in the library where he needed it.

Colorado State University has an Office of Instructional De–

---

*Auto–Instructional Media for Library Orientation

51

velopment which by means of grants encourages the development of innovative teaching techniques in the classroom. With the library serving as a classroom for the entire university population, we decided to apply for a grant with which to pursue a different approach to basic library instruction. After searching the literature for information on the subject and finding that information somewhat meager, we formed a project committee to prepare a grant proposal. It envisioned the use of self--service, point--of--need audiovisual units designed for individual instruction. Following approval by our Director of Public Services and the Director of Libraries, the University's Office of Instructional Development approved our request and awarded us some $2,000 for equipment and supplies. As its contribution to the project, the Libraries made available additional professional help at the reference desk to permit released time for members of the project committee. The members of the project committee* spent countless hours preparing the instructional programs, selecting appropriate audiovisual equipment, and planning for the evaluation of the project.

The outcome of our efforts (with valuable assistance from the University's Audio--Visual service, a statistical laboratory on campus, and our Librarian for Research and Development) was three instructional programs: one explaining the use of periodical indexes and how to locate periodicals in the library, another describing the use of the card catalog, and a third explaining the use of the *Monthly Catalog of U.S. Government Publications.* The programs average about five minutes in length and each is presented on a separate unit. Two of the units incorporate sound/slide equipment, and the third uses sound--only equipment. You will find a more detailed description of these units in appendix A. The units are located in the library's general reference area near the tools which they explain. To start the program, the patron need only lift a telephone handset mounted on the outside of the unit, which permits him to hear the program without disturbing others. Each program stops automatically at its conclusion and is ready to be played again when the handset is lifted. At the end of each program is an invitation to consult the reference librarian if additional help is needed.

Because the AIMLO units are designed for individual instruction and may be used at any hour the library is open, the question of how to evaluate their usefulness in an on--demand situation, rather than as a pre--scheduled classroom excercise, was a perplexing problem. We placed great value on the desirability of a hands--off policy, letting

---

*Barbara Aro, Betty Hacker, and Richard Stevens

the student decide when and if he wanted to use the machine, with no coercion or inquisitive follow–up by the library staff. At the same time we wanted to get some measure of the effectiveness of this type of instruction.

Initially we collected two types of data. First, a counter attached to each machine recorded each use. The counters were activated when the telephone receiver was lifted. Over a 14 month period, from November 1, 1971 to December 31, 1972, the counters recorded each use as follows:

TABLE 1

PERIODICAL INDEXES PROGRAM on	
3–M device	6,569 uses
CARD CATALOG PROGRAM on	
Carousel/Cousino device	3,834 uses
DOCUMENTS PROGRAM on	
Cousino (audio--only) device	1,912 uses
	12,315 TOTAL

The total, 12,315, was added to the total number of uses during a previous three week test period, that total being 1674. So a grand total of 13,989 uses was recorded during the 15 months of operation. Mathematically speaking, one could say that, at approximately 5 minutes per program, nearly four typical reference service months were covered on the AIMLO machines during the 15 month period. It is interesting to note that there was a coincidental drop in the number of questions asked at the general reference desk during fall quarter 1972, compared with fall quarter 1971.

The second type of data that we collected was from question–naires voluntarily filled out by students. These questionnaires, re–produced in appendix B, were placed in boxes adjacent to the ma–chines and a low–keyed appeal for the user's help in evaluating this kind of instruction was one of the last statements heard on each tape program. During the fourteen month period from November 1971 to December 1972, the questionnaire response rate was 4% of use for the periodical index program, 6% for the card catalog program, and 5% for the documents program. While these are not sufficient response rates to be statistically significant, it can be said that re–sponses to the questions which attempted to assess the value of this method of orientation indicated an almost total acceptance, in fact preference, for this method of instruction on the part of the respon–dents. Responses to questions 2, 4, 6, and 7 were overwhelmingly in favor of the program and the mechanical performance of the devices. The response to question number 8 was surprising in that students using the devices strongly preferred getting this kind of information through use of an audio–visual program and substantially preferred that means over asking a librarian. From question 9 we got interesting and enthusiastic comments, not only about the machines but about everything else in the library too. This was the first time we had asked a large group of students for any kind of comment about the library and the answers to these questions were unusually interesting for us.

During May, 1972, an attempt was made to assess the effectiveness of the AIMLO devices through the use of a telephone interview technique. A different questionnaire format was designed (appendix C) and these questionnaires replaced the regular ones during the month of May. A telephone interview form was devised to standardize the information sought during each interview. The response rate to this appeal was not substantial, only 30 (and even fewer, 16, agreed to a telephone interview). The information gained in the interviews gave further indication of the positive effectiveness of the programs when the respondents actually used the information they had learned from watching and/or listening to the programs.

In the summer of 1973, we decided upon a plan to evaluate the AIMLO instruction by means of a library use quiz administered to three sections of PY 100, the introductory psychology course. This particular class was chosen because of several factors. First of all, PY 100 is taken by many freshmen and the AIMLO programs were developed especially for freshmen. Secondly, the PY 100 register includes students from all of CSU's eight colleges, representing many different majors (69 major courses of study were represented by our sample population). Thirdly, the professor supervising all PY 100 sections had worked closely with our staff, understood our problem and intent, and she gained the cooperation of the instructors involved. The project began during the first week of October, 1973, soon after the opening of the fall quarter. Following our directions, the instructor of one PY 100 section urged his students to come to the library and use the AIMLO machines having programs on the card catalog and periodical indexes. A second psychology section received copies of printed guides to the library covering much of the information presented in the AIMLO programs, and these students were told to read the guides. The third PY 100 section received *no* library information. Nothing was mentioned about the library in that class. None of these sections were told about the forthcoming test.

On October eighth each of these sections was given the library use quiz (appendix D). A total of 502 students completed the quiz. In addition to the first five demographic and general questions on this library use quiz, the test consisted of 16 multiple choice questions, the answers to which were covered by both the printed guide and by the AIMLO programs.

The data from the test was analyzed using a canned program, the SPSS (Statistical Package for the Social Sciences). In this we were ably assisted by a member of the sociology faculty, a statistician with long experience in research methods. We were primarily interested in finding out the degree of success on the library use quiz, as between students having no previous instruction, instruction by the AIMLO machines, by the printed guide, by a librarian, and by a combination of several of these methods. We also wanted to see the scores of what we called "library use knowledge," based on three questions on the quiz which merely required geographical acquaintance with the building and services.

We probably should not have been as surprised as we were to discover that the directions given by the instructors in the three PY 100 sections had little or no effect on what the students actually did. For instance, of 196 students in the section assigned use of the machines, only 74 indicated that they had done so. As a matter of fact, 52.8% of the entire population tested indicated they had no exposure to any of the types of instruction.

For analysis, the respondents were divided into eight groups, according to their answers to questions one through three. Group I had no exposure to the instruction (52.8% of the population). Group II had been helped by a librarian (15.7%). Group III had read the printed guide (4.8%). Group IV had used the AIMLO machines (4.4%). Group V had been helped by a librarian and read the guides (8.6%). Group VI had been helped by a librarian and used the AIMLO machines (5.3%). Group VII had read the guides and used the machines (3%). Group VIII had used all three kinds of instruction (5%).

TABLE 2

MEAN SCORES ON LIBRARY USE QUIZ

GROUP I	(NO EXPOSURE)	7.5208	(8)
GROUP II	(LIBRARIAN)	8.9873	(5)
GROUP III	(GUIDES)	8.8750	(7)
GROUP IV	(MACHINES)	10.7727	(1)
GROUP V	(GUIDES & LIBRARIAN)	9.2093	(4)
GROUP VI	(MACHINES & LIBRARIAN)	8.9286	(6)
GROUP VII	(MACHINES & GUIDES)	9.4000	(3)
GROUP VIII	(MACHINES, GUIDES, LIBRARIAN)	9.8000	(2)

Table 2 shows the mean scores on the test, out of a possible perfect score of 16. As you can see, group IV, those students who had used the machines only, scored the highest. Groups VII and VIII which had used the machines and guides or all three types of instruction scored next highest. Of those students using only one type of instruction, the respondents having used the printed guide made the lowest score. The group with no exposure ranked last. The AIMLO machines appear in the top three categories, according to test results. That students may learn more from the audiovisual devices than from the printed word is indicated in the difference in scores between the group using only the machines and the group using only the guides.

Table 3 compares the groups on the basis of library use knowledge and library location knowledge. Groups having used the machines are still in the top two categories.

TABLE 3

MEAN SCORES -- LIBRARY USE KNOWLEDGE

GROUP I	(NO EXPOSURE)	5.8340	(8)
GROUP II	(LIBRARIAN)	6.9367	(5)
GROUP III	(GUIDES)	6.7500	(7)
GROUP IV	(MACHINES)	8.4545	(1)
GROUP V	(GUIDES & LIBRARIAN)	7.0465	(4)
GROUP VI	(MACHINES & LIBRARIAN)	6.8214	(6)
GROUP VII	(MACHINES & GUIDES)	7.3333	(2)
GROUP VIII	(MACHINES, GUIDES, LIBRARIAN)	7.1200	(3)

MEAN SCORES -- LIBRARY LOCATION KNOWLEDGE

GROUP I	(NO EXPOSURE)	1.6868	(8)
GROUP II	(LIBRARIAN)	2.0506	(7)
GROUP III	(GUIDES)	2.1520	(4)
GROUP IV	(MACHINES)	2.3182	(2)
GROUP V	(GUIDES & LIBRARIAN)	2.1628	(3)
GROUP VI	(MACHINES & LIBRARIAN)	2.1071	(5)
GROUP VII	(MACHINES & GUIDES)	2.0667	(6)
GROUP VIII	(MACHINES, GUIDES, LIBRARIAN)	2.6800	(1)

The technique used by our sociologist friend is called analysis of variance, which answers the question of whether there is a real difference, in this case between the scores of each group, or whether the results are due to chance. The analysis indicates that there is less than one chance in 10,000 that there is not a real difference. When the range of possible scores is only sixteen points, the difference between a score of seven and one of ten is significant.

There are two points which somewhat muddy the waters and if we were to rerun the test we would probably change these factors. First, the question about being helped by a librarian is vague and

56

subject to misinterpretation. Who, in the student's mind, *is* a librarian? It may be someone at the loan desk who helps him find a
book or tells him a book is overdue. And what constitutes "help?"
Secondly, we had no way to measure the students' prior knowledge
before use of the machine or other type of instruction.

As said at the outset, we were reluctant to become involved in a
strictly inforced testing program, but we feel that through the various kinds of evaluation methods used it can be shown that students
do learn from the AIMLO programs at least as well, and possibly
better, than from other kinds of instruction.

APPENDIX A

PROJECT AIMLO
COLORADO STATE UNIVERSITY

WHO: Colorado State University Libraries

WHAT: AIMLO (Auto–Instructional Media for Library Orientation)

WHEN: Funded by CSU Office of Instructional Development, May, 1971.
Programs developed and units assembled, Summer, 1971. In continuous use at CSU Libraries since September, 1971.

WHY: To provide self--service instruction in basic library techniques for patrons from a student body of 17,000. To provide information at the time and point of need. To supplement services of the reference staff.

HOW: Three self--contained units were designed: one audio-only device with message repeater (audio–announcer) – one sound--on--slide projector with recycler – one slide projector with message repeater -- and cabinets to house each unit. Programs were written to explain use of the card catalog, of periodical indexes, and of the Monthly Catalog of U.S. Publications. Colored slides were prepared to illustrate the programs. Audio–visual programs depict a dialogue between an inquiring student and the reference librarian; audio--only programs are narrated by the reference librarian. Programs are activated when the user lifts a telephone receiver, and automatically recycle. Length of program is 5 to 9 minutes. The instructional units are placed near their appropriate points of use.

HOW MUCH:

Equipment

Unit 1 – Kodak Ektagraphic slide projector with 3 inch lens
Orrtronics Audio Announcer Syncro--Re--peater and accessories $428.10

Unit 2 -- 3--M model 525 Projector–Recorder (Sound--on--Slide) with 3 inch lens, Model 325 Recycle Unit, slide tray and accessories   888.00

Unit 3 -- Orrtronics Audio Announcer Repeater and accessories   126.95

Cabinets for above (custom--built, total for all 3 units)   364.05

58

Supplies (slides, electric cord, etc.)   100.00
                                          TOTAL $1,907.10

WHAT
RESULTS: Evaluation forms voluntarily filled out by students show
           high level of interest, understanding of programs, and
           receptive attitude toward new media. Automatic coun-
           ters, recording each use of unit, indicate usage signifi-
           cantly exceeding expectations. Mechanical performance
           has proved to be excellent, with few technical problems.
WHAT
NEXT: Plans include development of new programs, covering
           additional research sources, and based in part on re--
           quests by users; possible acquisition of new teaching
           units for other areas of the library.
WHERE: COLORADO STATE UNIVERSITY LIBRARIES,
           FORT COLLINS, COLORADO 80521
           Contact: Richard C. Stevens, Betty Hacker, or Barbara
           Aro 303--491--5911

COLORADO STATE UNIVERSITY LIBRARIES
KEYS TO CSU LIBRARIES

This opportunity for self--instruction in the use of the library was made possible by a grant from the CSU Office of Instructional Development. It involves NO FUNDS from the CSU Libraries' budget. By completing this questionnaire, you will help us evaluate this type of library instruction.

Please mark squares with an X to record your answers ( )

0. In what category are you? Please mark one.

freshman	sophomore	junior	senior	graduate student
1.	2.	3.	4.	5.
faculty	staff	other		
6.	7.	8.		

1. What best describes your reason for listening to this program? Please mark one.
    1. for curiosity satisfaction
    2. for general information
    3. for specific information (for term paper, etc.)
    4. for class assignment to use this program
    5. other
2. Did you understand this program?
    1. yes
    2. no
    3. not completely
3. How much of the information presented did you already know?
    1. none
    2. some
    3. most
    4. all
4. Do you think you will find this program helpful in using the library?
    1. yes
    2. no
    3. somewhat
5. How many times did you watch this program today?
    1. once
    2. twice
    3. more
6. Did you enjoy this program?
    1. yes
    2. no

3.   no comment
7. How did you find the mechanical performance of this device?
    1.   satisfactory
    2.   unsatisfactory
8. How would you prefer to get this kind of information about the library? Please mark one.
    1.   watching or listening to this kind of program
    2.   asking a friend
    3.   reading a library handbook
    4.   asking a librarian
9. Please feel free to use this space and the back for any additional comments which may help us evaluate this type of library instruction.

COLORADO STATE UNIVERSITY LIBRARIES

KEYS TO CSU LIBRARIES

This opportunity for self--instruction in the use of the library was made possible by a grant from the CSU Office of Instructional De--velopment. It involves NO FUNDS from the CSU Libraries' budget. By completing this questionnaire, you will help us evaluate this type of library instruction.

Please mark squares with an X to record your answers ( ).
Please return the questionnaire to the box nearby.

0. In what category are you? Please mark one.

freshman	sophomore	junior	senior	graduate student
1.	2.	3.	4.	5.
faculty	staff	other		
6.	7.	8.		

1. How much of the information presented in this program did you already know?

none	some	most	all
1.	2.	3.	4.

2. Do you think you will find this program helpful in using the library?

yes	no	somewhat
1.	2.	3.

3. Would you be willing to participate further in an evaluation of this type of library instruction, by allowing a short telephone inter--view with a member of the library staff?

yes	no
1.	2.

If *yes*, please give your name:
    tel. no.:
What is the best time to reach you at this number? Day
                                                    Hour

THANK YOU VERY MUCH!

APPENDIX D – LIBRARY USE QUIZ

This quiz is intended to assist the library staff in evaluating and im-- proving services available at the Wm. E. Morgan Library. Your co-- operation is appreciated.

Check one answer for each of the following questions:

1. Have you used the auto--instructional (slide/tape) machines located in the first floor lobby of the Library?   Yes   No
2. Have you read the sections of the printed "Guide to the Libraries" which explain use of the card catalog and how to locate periodicals?   Yes   No
3. Have you been helped to use the Library by one of the librarians?   Yes   No
4. In what category are you?   Freshman   Soph.   Junior   Senior   Grad.   Other
5. What is your major?   (Write in answer)

Following are some questions about the *Morgan Library at C.S.U.* Please check one answer for each question:

6. The C.S.U. card catalog is divided into more than one major section. How many?
   a) Six
   b) Two
   c) Three
7. The card catalog is located on the:
   a) first floor near the loan desk.
   b) first floor near the reference desk.
   c) second floor.
8. If you know only the title of a book,
   a) you could still find it in the card catalog by looking for the title.
   b) you would have to find out the author's name first, to find it in the card catalog.
   c) you could only find it in the card catalog by looking under the subject of the book.
9. When you look in the card catalog for books listed under a subject heading,
   a) cards for the most recently published books under that subject will be filed first.
   b) cards for the most recently published books under that subject will be filed last.
   c) all cards under that subject are filed alphabetically.

10. You can find out the number of pages in a book from informa-- tion given on the catalog card,
    a) usually.
    b) sometimes.
    c) rarely.
11. Catalog cards contain information about the subjects covered by a book,
    a) in the upper, right–hand corner of the card.
    b) immediately following the title.
    c) near the bottom of the card.
12. To find the *title* "The History of Henry Fielding" in the card catalog, you should look under the word:
    a) The
    b) History
    c) Fielding
13. The call number for a book or periodical is found:
    a) in the center bottom of the catalog card.
    b) in the lower left--hand corner of the catalog card.
    c) in the upper left--hand corner of the catalog card.
14. Most books at C:S.U. are classified in the
    a) Library of Congress classification system.
    b) Dewey Decimal system.
    c) Universal Decimal classification system.
15. Which of the following is a Dewey Decimal classification call number?
    a) 611/B18s.
    b) 67–6229.
    c) TN144/B47/1959.
16. Which of the following is a Library of Congress classification call number?
    a) TN/144/B47/1959.
    b) 611/B18s.
    c) 67–6229.
17. At C.S.U., the word FOLIO in a call number means:
    a) an unbound periodical.
    b) a large size book or large size periodical.
    c) a bound volume of a periodical.
18. To find out exactly which volumes of a periodical the Library owns, you would go to:
    a) the periodical indexes.
    b) the serials record.
    c) the shelves where the volumes are.
19. To receive help in using the periodical indexes, the best place to ask is at:
    a) the loan desk.

b) the reserve desk.

c) a reference desk.

20. Many of the most recent periodicals are shelved:

    a) in the periodicals room.

    b) at the reserve desk.

    c) on the slanted display shelves.

21. Materials on microtext are located:

    a) in a room behind the loan desk.

    b) on the shelves with other books.

    c) at the reserve desk.

EVALUATION ATTEMPTS OF LIBRARY USE INSTRUCTION PROGRAMS AT THE UNIVERSITY OF COLORADO LIBRARIES

John Lubans, Jr.
Assistant Director for Public Services
University of Colorado Libraries

Introduction[1]

Instructional programs in all types of libraries have been in--frequently evaluated. Their need and effect have not been measured except in a few isolated cases. When measurement or evaluation has taken place it has been largely heuristic, that is, not scientifically established but useful nevertheless to explain observations made in library use instruction. There are few statistically valid studies but these deal with methods of instruction rather than the success or lack of success on the part of the user in learning about information use.

The evaluations that have been done reflect to a certain extent the prevalent uncertainty that exists around what the objectives of library use instruction are or should be.

Most library use instruction is based on what we as librarians *think* library users need to know. It is this educated guesswork or perceived need on which many programs (tours, orientation lectures, a multitude of multimedia presentations and formal courses in bib--liography) have been based. Since we are prompted to action by what we observe as lacking in the library users at the time of the user's need, our response is apt to be a type of bibliographic first aid. This may explain some of the lack of long range objectives in edu--cating the library user. That there is a need for library instruction can be vouchsafed by most librarians working with the public. Probably the major errors in basing programs only on perceived need is the redundancy inherent in such an approach and that such a shortsighted view does not generally get to the source of many in--formation use problems: The teacher/librarian relationship. In--variably the beginning user gets the greatest amount of attention, with little offered to the slightly advanced user. This situation is changing somewhat and evaluation of programs (including surveys of user/non--user needs) will do much to redirect instruction -- in col--laboration with the teacher -- towards the other levels where it can be substantive.

We should be able to measure the impact of instruction. The results of evaluation not only present possible alternatives for better programs but also should provide some standards of performance for such instruction and serve as a means to demonstrate to funding agencies the role of libraries in effective information use.

Problems of Evaluation

We may be able to measure the immediate effects of library use instruction but have no means at present to measure the long range, lasting effect. For that matter the short term result is just as difficult to grasp since very few school, public or academic librarians get to see the completed research paper or report or whatever the end result may be of the question on which they assisted the user. Even in the school environment few librarians are consulted by teachers re--garding the bibliographic quality of research papers.

Another problem of evaluation, particularly when the user is asked for his opinion, is the user's almost certain lack of experience (and resulting inability) with which to effectively compare one learning situation with another. He can react to what is at hand, that is, did it help when he needed it, but generally has little under--standing of the broader perspectives of information use.

One particular concern in use instruction is the apparent re--dundancy and lack of retention on the part of the user. It is not uncommon for a person to be instructed in the use of the *Readers' Guide* several times during his student life and for him to never re--tain the information. As a research paper deadline approaches the library instruction cycle restarts. This is indicative of the lack of continuity in library user education and of the uneven emphasis on bibliographic skills by classroom teachers.

A study[2] of library use instruction at a high school and its feeder schools concluded that instruction offered by these schools was not developmental (that is, it did not build and expand upon skills previously taught) and that instruction tended to be concen--trated at one or two grade levels. Since it is likely these conditions are a result of a lack of a strong and consistent identity for library use in the curriculum, this role should be emphasized in planning library user education programs.

Evaluation Attempts at the University of Colorado

The University of Colorado Libraries offer a variety of pro--grams directed at educating the library user. There are over a dozen such identifiable attempts made. The range from an effort that recognizes the ebb and flow of a students life called the *Term Paper Clinic* to three formal bibliography courses to multi--media pro--grams.

We've felt some need to evaluate which way our efforts were headed since the diversity and number of programs we offer are highly time--consuming -- on occasion we think if we have any more demand for this type of program there will not be staff to carry it. Also, we're certain that evaluation will show user appreciation to our efforts and also the demand and need for added services. This is a valuable aid in budget hearings when we are in competition with other university departments. Evaluation takes us beyond the library as an institution "entitled" to its slice of the money and, hope--fully, out of the "bottomless pit" budgetary concept. As you all know, the philosophy of libraries being akin to motherhood and the flag is coming increasingly under fire.

The first evaluation is of two media (slide/tape) presentations entitled "How to find a book" and "How to find a periodical" (Evaluation Questionnaire I). It reveals in the first question that most of the viewers found them "helpful." Most of the comments and reactions could be expected. However, Question 5 (Which of the following types of programs would you prefer?) has some inter--esting responses. A group approaching one--half of the respondents feels the need for shorter programs on more specific topics.

This evaluation, particularly the comments, resulted in new editions of these programs being produced -- shortened programs, with different and more lively music, and a new narrator. (Because of observed mechanical difficulties, we have gone to an easily oper--ated filmstrip cassette approach versus the previously clumsy and erratic slide/tape arrangement).

Evaluation Questionnaires II--A&B deal with the short, point of need film loop on how to use the *Readers' Guide*. Apart from learning the full title of the *Readers' Guide* and the placement of the apostrophe in the word *Readers'*, the evaluation of this film pointed out some interesting things -- particularly about whether or not the student "learned" (Question 1). This film was done at the Univer--sity of Colorado as an experiment -- also a few other colleges heard about it and purchased copies. One of them (Moraine Valley Com--munity College in Illinois) agreed to do a similar evaluation, using the same questionnaire as used at the University of Colorado. There were 53 respondents to the University of Colorado questionnaire over a six month period in 1972 and a response of 99 in the Moraine Valley evaluation. Although these two can probably not be scien--tifically compared, the results are sometimes similar. Differences in the two responses appear in Question 1 and the number definitely stating they weren't helped by the film in learning about the *Readers' Guide*.

There is a strong contrast in Question 5 in regard to being able to stop and start the film. This may be due to the heavy influence of media in community college learning resource centers. Also, there is a similar contrast in Question 6 about background music and narration.

Evaluation III deals with the written response of one group of students who have taken *Dissertation Acupuncture* which is offered by the library through the Continuing Education department and taught by as many as eight librarians. Originally, it was concerned with the student at the dissertation--writing level, but now we have begun accepting master's level students. The reactions of the students are favorable and several point another direction librarians should be taking -- i.e., the teaching of *all* graduate research methods (literature use) classes.

Another study undertaken at the University of Colorado dealt with trying to ascertain student needs in knowing how to use li--braries. Some selected tables from this study are shown as Eval--uation IV. It cites the reaction of 370 non--users and users. (139 respondents termed themselves non--users and the remainder were users).

Table IV--A looks at the way library users and non--users see libraries. Undoubtedly, both conceptual and institutional images are involved in the responses. This table is arranged by user and non--user agreement or disagreement. There are 5 statements following the opening remark of "when I walk into a library I feel . . . ":

1. relaxed.
   Some agreement but more disagreement on this point, particularly from the non--user (54 percent) which is odd since he supposedly never comes in the library. This may be part of the problem. Quite a bit of neutrality on both sides.
2. curious.
   Agreement, particularly by the user at 50 percent.
3. purposeful.
   Both the non--user and user have a mission in their visit to the library as revealed by the scores of 61 percent and 78 percent.
4. frustrated.
   Some surprising agreement on this point. Is this in anti--cipation of problems that will occur?
5. cooped up.
   The high agreement here (58 and 45 percent) may be a local problem. The central library at University of Colorado is fairly old, unmodular and poorly ventilated or this may indicate some historical problems on the user's part. Perhaps it is the idea of working under frustrating conditions under pressure because of pending due dates

for course work.

There is something here for the architects. Openness and rapid access are necessary according to both users and non--users.

The next table (Table IV–B) shows what the user/non--user considers valuable to a student regardless of his subject area. The table is arranged by non--users and users in percentages under the headings: agree, neutral, disagree, and don't know.

1. knowledge of . . . agreement
2. awareness of pertinent literature . . . agreement
3. knowledge of how to . . . agreement
4. knowledge of one or more languages . . . split decision

The first three categories reveal strong support among students of what may be considered the objectives of library use instruction. But then this may be what the student recommends for *other* students and not necessarily for himself. However, if these are some of the objectives of educating library users then it does indicate at least in principle that we are on firm ground. The response as indicated in the next table (IV–C) shows even more direct sentiment among the user/non--user as to the value of instruction in library use.

One section of the questionnaire dealt with certain library services/facilities that the respondent may have used (e.g. card catalog, reference books, etc.). The next table (IV–D) shows the results in percentages for non--users and users when asked why they didn't make use of particular library services/facilities.

The major reason (31 and 44 percent) given is because both the non--user and user "felt no need for them."

The next major reason is that they didn't know these services/facilities existed (25 and 21 percent respectively).

This last reason when taken with the percentages who couldn't locate the service (15 and 11 percent) indicates the problem the user has when faced with library use. First, he doesn't necessarily know about the service and, on the occasion he does, he can't find it some of the time.

The final table (IV--E) deals with three topics:

1. how the faculty member and his view of library use are perceived by the user/non--user.
2. what the user thinks of his knowledge of library use.
3. what the library can do about helping the user/non--user make better use of the library's resources.

First, about the teaching faculty member. One reason for non–use is discovered in the percentage response to comment 1, to which 51 percent of the non--users and 32 percent of the users do not feel that their courses involve using the library.

There is in item 2 general disagreement (51 and 45 percent) that library use skills are taken into account in grades by the teaching faculty. At the same time, there is quite a bit (30 percent) of neutrality or ignorance on the topic.

Statement 3 received a strong affirmative response that the teaching faculty assume some expertise in library use on the part of the student. This contradicts the librarian's on the job experience. (Perhaps the faculty's assumptions are not all that high.)

In response to what the user thinks of his won abilities in information use, there are some contradictory findings. "Are you at a loss . . . " receives some agreement but more disagreement. Yet the next item, number 4, shows strong common sentiment of feeling there are information resources the user/non–user has missed somehow.

The answer to whether or not the user/non--user feels well able to do research in the library (number 6) shows some concern on the part of the respondents, as revealed by the "disagree" column (44 and 23 percent). This is in fact quite low -- at least one study shows the users perception of his abilities as far exceeding reality.

The role of the library is given some guidelines by the respondents when they suggest the library should offer sources, clinics, etc. in library use (61 and 64 percent respectively). However, the taking advantage of these courses is another matter. But, although there is a drop in the total figure, 38 percent and 43 percent would avail themselves of such opportunities.

We plan additional evaluation at the University of Colorado not only on finding the best methods of instruction, but also of the impact of our instructional efforts on students in view of certain established objectives. Extensive evaluation is underway in our CLR-NEH grant program and our plan is to directly involve the student/ faculty participants in this program over a period of at least two years.

REFERENCES

[1]*Introduction* and *Problems of Evaluation* taken from the draft of Lubans, John Jr., "Evaluating Library User Education Programs" in *Educating the Library User*, edited by John Lubans, Jr. (N.Y.: R.R. Bowker, 1974) Copyright, R.R. Bowker Co.

[2]Louise Crosby and Sherril Totemeier, "Library Skills Instruction at Alameda Senior High School and Its Feeder Schools; Is It De-- velopmental?" Research Paper. (Graduate School of Librarianship, University of Denver, 1971).

Evaluation
Questionnaire I

University of Colorado – 1971

QUESTIONNAIRE ON SLIDE/TAPE PROGRAMS
(responses to 27 questionnaires tallied)

1   Did you find the slide/tape programs helpful?
    yes – 25 (2, "slightly")
    no – 2
2. What did you like about the programs?
    "Short and to the point; good directions."
    "They served their purpose."
    "It really spelled things out, and with a bit of humor; kept my
    attention."
3. What did you *not* like about the programs?
    "Too much information presented in too short a time. The
    periodical program had no review at the end as it should
    have." (2)
    "They were quite boring; the voice was irritating." (2)
    "Not enough information on the actual structure of the
    library." (3)
    "The sick music in the background and sitting in the middle of
    a hallway listening to it." (3)
4. Were they too long?
    yes – 4
    no – 23
5. Which of the following types of programs would you prefer.
    (check one)
    11   a) six or seven shorter programs on more specific topics
         such as the card catalog, the *Catalog of Serials*, the classi-
         fication systems, etc.
     0   b) one short introduction to the library omitting the
         details of how you actually locate materials.
    16   c) the two programs as they are or with slight modifications.
6. What changes would you make in the programs now on the
    machine?
    "More directions in periodicals tape." (2)
    "Fix volume control on periodicals program."
    "Get the machines away from the copier."
    "Show structure of library; more on classification system." (4)
    "Possibly go through a few more examples of finding some-
    thing."
    "More information about branch libraries would be helpful."

"Change speaker's voice; some slides were awfully bright to sit close to."

7. What other ideas would you like to see implemented in teaching use of the library?

"More tours and information booths."

"I think the tours should be lengthened especially trying to determine how to find materials in the upper tiers."

"Film strips on various subjects displayed in a viewer for any interested student to see."

UNIVERSITY OF COLORADO LIBRARIES
The Readers' Guide: How To Use It
Questionnaire

Percentages
Please fill this out. It will help us improve our services.
1. Did you learn how to use the *Readers' Guide* after viewing this
   film. (Please mark the most appropriate answer.)
   45   Yes, I did learn.
   33   Yes, I learned some things but still have questions.
   22   No, the film didn't help me learn.
        If No, please explain why:

2. Have you ever used the *Readers' Guide* elsewhere? (for example
   in high school)
   78 Yes   22 No
   If Yes, do any of the following apply after seeing the film:
   16   I learned things about it I didn't know before.
   58   The program refreshed my memory about using it.
   26   I didn't learn anything I didn't already know.
3. How interesting was this program.
   38   Very interesting.
   58   Interesting.
        O.K.
        Dull.
   6   Very dull.
4. Was the program   10   too long,   23   too short or,   67
   just right.
5. Would it have helped to be able to stop the program at certain
   places or to repeat certain parts?   36 Yes   64 No
6. Do you think the film would have been better with narration and
   background music?   39 Yes   61 No
7. How would you prefer to get information about library tools?
   60   Watching this kind of program.
   6   Asking a friend.
   8   Reading about it.
   28   Asking a librarian.
8. How could this program be improved:

THANKS. Please leave this questionnaire in box by the projector.

Evaluation
Questionnaire II–B
Moraine Valley

UNIVERSITY OF COLORADO LIBRARIES
The Readers' Guide: How To Use It
Questionnaire

Percentages
Please fill this out. It will help us improve our services.
1. Did you learn how to use the *Readers' Guide* after viewing this
   film. (Please mark the most appropriate answer.)
   55   Yes, I did learn.
   0   Yes, I learned some things but still have questions.
   44   No, the film didn't help me learn.
   If No, please explain why:

2. Have you ever used the *Readers' Guide* elsewhere? (for example,
   in high school)
   66   Yes   22   No   11   did not answer
   If Yes, do any of the following apply after seeing the film:
   14   I learned things about it I didn't know before.
   56   The program refreshed my memory about using it.
   28   I didn't learn anything I didn't already know.
3. How interesting was this program.
        Very interesting.
        Interesting.
   88   O.K.
   11   Dull.
        Very dull.
4. Was the program 0 too long, 33 too short, or 66 just right.
5. Would it have helped to be able to stop the program at certain
   places or to repeat certain parts? 66 Yes   33 No
6. Do you think the film would have been better with narration and
   background music?
   66 Yes   33 No
7. How would you prefer to get information about library tools?
   88   Watching this kind of program.
        Asking a friend.
        Reading about it.
   11   Asking a librarian.
8. How could this program be improved:

THANKS. Please leave this questionnaire in box by the projector.

UNIVERSITY OF COLORADO LIBRARIES

Student Evaluation of Dissertation Acupuncture
(advanced bibliography course)

It is paramount to a researcher to know the library and its materials as a librarian does, and the course this summer was an excellent beginning.

*I feel that this course could be improved by holding it at some time later than 7:00 a.m.

It seems to me that the material presented in these sessions should be presented by the senior library staff who conducted these sessions for the "Dissertation Acupuncture," for their knowledge of their material can't be matched easily within department ranks . . .

Now I'm finally beginning to feel secure that I can find the information I need systematically and quickly thanks to all of you. I hadn't realized that so many tools and facilities are available or even how to go about finding what and if specific types of information are readily available to me.

However, the information regarding known topic sources could be incorporated in the various departmental research methods course to reduce the time spent in the initial topic selection process.

Many students believe that there is little to learn about how to use the library. Thus, a substantive outline of proposed course content might be published on your next announcement/enrollment flyer.

UNIVERSITY OF COLORADO LIBRARIES

IV--A. *PERCENTAGES*

	Agree		Neutral		Disagree		Don't Know	
	non–user	user	non–user	user	non–user	user	non–user	user

When I walk into a library I feel:

1. Relaxed, want to pick up an interesting book and read.

non–user	user	non–user	user	non–user	user	non–user	user
20	34	22	24	54	39	4	3

2. Curious, want to browse through the books.

non–user	user	non–user	user	non–user	user	non–user	user
39	50	15	18	44	29	3	0

3. Purposeful, want to do some serious work.

non–user	user	non–user	user	non–user	user	non–user	user
61	78	12	14	25	8	2	0

4. Frustrated, want to get what I need without being there half a day.

non–user	user	non–user	user	non–user	user	non–user	user
67	50	16	13	15	30	2	6

5. Cooped--up, want to get outside and breathe deeply.

non–user	user	non–user	user	non–user	user	non–user	user
58	45	17	25	20	35	4	4

IV--B. Each of the following I consider valuable to a student regardless of his study areas:

Agree		Neutral		Disagree		Don't Know	
non–user	user	non–user	user	non–user	user	non–user	user

Knowledge of use of bibliographies abstracts, and indexes.

non–user	user	non–user	user	non–user	user	non–user	user
77	80	10	9	11	9	3	2

Awareness of pertinent literature in fields related to his own field.

non–user	user	non–user	user	non–user	user	non–user	user
84	87	8	7	8	5	1	0

Knowledge of how to look for specific information.

non–user	user	non–user	user	non–user	user	non–user	user
89	93	3	4	7	3	1	0

Knowledge of one or more foreign languages.

non–user	user	non–user	user	non–user	user	non–user	user
30	34	30	27	30	35	8	3

Evaluation IV Cont'd.

IV--C. Knowing how to use the library is over--rated. You can get along without instruction in library use.

Percentages

Agree		Neutral		Disagree		Don't Know	
non--user	user	non--user	user	non--user	user	non--user	user
24	21	17	15	53	60	6	4

IV--D. Regarding the library services/facilities you have not used, was it because you:

non--user	user	
25	21	didn't know they even existed
7	9	were aware of them but didn't have time
12	7	didn't want to ask about how to use them
31	44	felt no need to use them
10	6	figured it wasn't worth the time spent using them
1	1	thought only librarians were supposed to use them
15	11	couldn't locate the service even though I knew it existed

IV--E

Disagree		Agree	
non--user	user	non--user	user

1. Do assignments in your courses usually involve using library resources other than just books placed on reserve by professors?

51	32	48	68

2. Is your expertise or lack of it in library use taken into account by your professors when they grade your papers?

51	45	8	10

3. Do instructors assume that you already know enough about using the libraries to do an in--depth term paper?

4	6	81	79

4. Are you at a loss when faced with doing a term paper in the library?

35	53	41	23

	Disagree		Agree	
	non–user	user	non–user	user

5. Whenever you do a research paper in the library do you get a feeling that there are information resources on your topic which you are somehow missing?

4	12	80	76

6. Do you feel well able to do research in the library?

44	23	34	62

7. Do you think that the library should offer courses, clinics, etc. in how to use libraries and their resources?

30	7	61	64

8. Would you take such courses, clinics, etc. if offered at a convenient time?

25	24	38	43

*Totals of less than 100% represent a response of "don't know" or "neutral."

COMMENTS ON LIBRARY INSTRUCTION PROGRAMS
AND EVALUATIONS

Dr. Rowena Weiss Swanson
University of Denver Graduate School of Librarianship

I would like to comment briefly about questionnaire design and library instruction programs, but I would like to preface my remarks concerning these two items with a comment about evaluation methodology itself. I think one cannot conduct an evaluation of any program without having a knowledge of evaluation methodology. We can't make jokes about our ignorance in this area or talk about our ignorance as though it were a virtue. It is my belief that we do not know, and we have to know, we must learn. For most of us who have completed our academic training, this means that we have to teach ourselves. Although my degrees don't include one in librarianship, I have treated librarianship as I have treated a number of other subjects, as subjects that I have had to learn a lot about before I have entered the ballparks of those particular disciplines.

Evaluation is a type of scientific inquiry that can profitably employ a variety of tools and techniques of scientific methodology. Those of you who are interested in conducting evaluation should learn how to use at least some of these tools and techniques. In this regard I want to suggest a book that I have found very useful: Ed-- ward Suchman's *Evaluative Research*[1]. It provides quite a lot of detail on evaluation methodology and is, at the same time, highly readable. As I recall, Suchman is not going to help you with different kinds of sample designs and it is not going to help with different kinds of questionnaire designs, but it will give you a perspective overview of evaluation methodology. For questions on sample designs, I would recommend *Survey Sampling* by Leslie Kish[2] as eminently readable and informative.

Parenthetically, I might add that I think librarianship is a very difficult profession in which to work because it seems to me that librarianship requires the acquisition of knowledge of many subject areas each of which would entitle one to consider himself a professional if he acquired that knowledge. While obviously no one of us can obtain complete knowledge of all relevant subject areas, we have to acquire some substantive knowledge of the subject areas we are concerned with if we are going to perform effectively. Two increasingly important companion areas to librarianship are scientific research and behavioral science. Perhaps it is unrealistic to consider reading many books in these areas, but certainly some study is necessary if one is to engage in evaluation or to provide library and information services.

In the realm of person--to--person interaction that arises in supervision and management and in communicating with patrons, it is beneficial to know about possible behavior patterns of people so that they can be anticipated with the possible end result of better meeting their needs.

With respect to library instruction program design, one must, first of all, address the objective one wishes to accomplish with the program. Some of the instruction programs may, for example, have the purpose of teaching the acquisition of library skills to people who completely lack such skills. What teaching approach is to be employed? All too often, it is rote drill, but behavioral science has shown that this technique does not promote transferrable learning. Many of the instructional programs that have been discussed during this meeting appear to me to be in the rote drilling category. I would like to underscore that a certain amount of rote drilling may be necessary, but I think that librarians who have to teach college students and others about how to use different library resources so that they can then apply this knowledge ought also to think about the possible needs for library resources these people will be having, and the instruction program should be embedded in the context of these anticipated needs. I don't know how nonsimilar you may think academic librarianship is to school librarianship, but the literature of school librarianship shows, during the last ten years or so, how school librarians have begun to think of integrating library instruction with educational programs. I suggest that there is much in the school library literature on library instruction program integration that can be adapted to college and university students' library needs.

As to questionnaire design, why aren't students interested in responding to your questionnaires (as reflected by low response percentages)? If I try to project myself back to the position of an undergraduate in a university, I would say, and forgive me for using the CSU questionnaire as an example, that I might have looked on it as insulting my intelligence. It looks to me to be too simplistic, too trivial, too unrelated to anything I am in the university for. Now as a student, my judgement about this questionnaire may be 100% wrong, but whether I am wrong or not, if the end result is that I am not going to answer the questionnaire, you haven't reached me. If the whole game of your effort is to reach me, then you had better find out what turns me on. I think that student response to ques--

tionnaires such as the CSU questionnaire points out all too well a problem in the area of understanding patron needs and being able to have meaningful communication with patrons.

With respect to the University of Colorado questionnaires, I think we find another problem. While the CU questionnaires re-- garding the rote drills on the *Readers' Guide* might not turn me off as a student, I find that I am turned off as a researcher trying to acquire planning or evaluation data for my instructional program. Why? I don't get enough information from these questionnaires to permit me to do very much planning or evaluation. If my data collection instrument does not give me enough data to perform an adequate analysis, as a researcher I must ask myself whether the re-- search excercise is worth doing. On CU evaluation IV, we have heard from Dr. Johnson and others about the relationship between the phrasing of questions and the nature of the responses to those ques-- tions. Question design studies teach that one has to be extremely careful in the wording of questions to avoid phraseology that may be self--serving, phrasing that tends to indicate the kinds of responses the researcher appears to want. In English or in any other natural language, it's not easy to get precision of expression, but to the de-- gree possible, we have to try to formulate questions that are not self-- serving and that have a high likelihood of yielding some kind of ob-- jective truth. The CU questionnaire labeled IV--A really doesn't tell me anything. It's too unspecific to provide substantive information and I read it as being self--serving. I'd like also to mention IV--B because I look at IV--B as providing a different kind of information. The questions in IV--B are certainly valid, but for what purpose? I read IV--B as furnishing general attitudinal responses. Certainly be-- fore one works with a population it is advisable to have some back-- ground information about that population's attitudes on the topic of inquiry. To a large extent, unfortunately, we still don't know very much about users' attitudes. I recently reread the book co--authored by Leonard, Maier, and Dougherty entitled *Centralized Book Pro-- cessing*[3]. One of the chapters in that book is a report on an ac-- ademic library user attitude survey that is very good and well worth reading. Although I don't have any quantitative proof, I have a hunch that the user attitudes described in the CBP study are very typical of user attitudes that one will find in a lot of academic en-- vironments in the United States. But before we can start querying users and nonusers, before we can begin to design instruction pro-- grams that are likely to meet with a high response from our actual and potential patron populations, we have to know to some extent what's in our users' heads about their image of us and of our ability to be of service to them.

Time doesn't permit an extensive discussion of questionnaire design, possible purposes of library instruction programs, research methodology for program evaluations, and possible strategies in the development of library instruction programs for university students' needs. As a commentator at this meeting, I have tried merely to set before you a few issues. In closing, I think it important to emphasize that evaluation should not be viewed as a one--shot excercise. Sometimes our managements and research sponsors don't like to hear us say that to accomplish an end result, we must first develop a pre-liminary or trial program; perform a preliminary evaluation; and then proceed through several iterations -- with all these steps consuming time, money, and personnel -- before we can be expected to have a stable, tried--and--true product. The resource cost that this involves is difficult to get accepted. Perhaps we also have to learn a bit about aggressive salesmanship! However, the keepers of the pursestrings, hopefully, are becoming a little more knowledgeable as to the resource requirements of library program and product development. In any event, it is dubious that library instruction programs and evaluations that aren't well planned and soundly designed and executed are worth such investment as is made in them.

REFERENCES

[1]Suchman, Edward. *Evaluative Research.* New York: Russell Sage Foundation, 1967.
[2]Kish, Leslie. *Survey Sampling.* New York: Wiley, 1965.
[3]Leonard, Lawrence, Joan Maier, and Richard Dougherty. *Central-- ized Book Processing.* Metuchen, N.J.: Scarecrow Press, 1969.

EVALUATION IN THE INSTRUCTIONAL PSYCHOLOGY MODEL

Marvin E. Wiggins
General Reference Librarian
Brigham Young University

The development of highly effective library use instruction programs may require expertise in library science, instructional psychology, electronic media, television production, the discipline for which
the instruction is being written, and statistical analysis.   Should a
library be fortunate enough to get someone on its staff containing
all this expertise, it would be blessed indeed. Yet, this expertise does
exist on most college campuses and until we get it ourself, and/or on
our staff, librarians could assemble that collective expertise contained
in all of these areas and produce superior products. It is when we try
to play one or more of these roles for which we are not professionally
trained, that we produce inferior products.

I come to you today as a librarian with particular training and
expertise in library science and as a collaborator with experts from
those *fields* mentioned above in the development of five basic library use instructional programs. These programs have been found
to be statistically valid and to guarantee a high level of learning on
those objectives agreed by the library and our English Composition
Department to be relevant to the freshman and sophomore curriculum on our campus. Mr. Blaine Hall, a holder of Masters Degrees in
both English Literature and Library Science, was selected by the
English Composition Department to give advise at all levels of the
program and to help see that instruction was relevant to their curriculum. The expertise and personnel in the evaluation came mainly
from our Instructional Research and Development Department. If
you have read my articles in July 1972 issue of *Drexel Library
Quarterly,*[1] the November 1972 issue of *College and Research Libraries,*[2] and the 1973 Pierian Press publication *A Challenge for
Academic Libraries*[3] then, you might remember that our library instruction has been based on an instructional design which guarantees
a high level of validity and learning. It is the steps we as a development team went through in the evaluation phase of this design which
I will discuss in this presentation.

In the summer of 1970, the reference personnel of the Clark

Library made the decision to turn to the expertise among the university faculty in forming a series of five basic library use instructional programs for lower division students to be administered within the English Composition curriculum. We organized a team of librarians, English instructors, instructional psychologists, and nonprint media experts to examine the library instruction needs of the lower division student.

We concluded that freshman and sophomore students needed certain library skills, and such skills were more basic than those needed by junior, senior, and graduate students. A philosophical decision was made to emphasize only that instruction needed at the particular level of the curriculum for which it was to be administered. We concluded that we would begin with a foundation of five basic instructional packages including: 1) an audio tape cassette tour, 2) use of the card catalog, 3) use of general periodical indexes, 4) use of basic book and newspaper indexes, and 5) use of basic indexes to U.S. government documents. The first four of these programs are now developed. The last program on government documents has been awaiting the arrival of the Carrollton Press publication: *Cumulative Subject Index to the Monthly Catalog.* With the first volume of this index now available and others promised shortly, we should be able to develop this program soon. When all programs are completed, they will be published as a single volume for national distribution. The exception will be the library tour which is applicable only to the Clark Library but is available for a $2.00 reproduction fee from my office as a model for similar tours in other libraries.

After these basic programs are developed, we plan to expand to an application of these definitions, concepts, and rules by teaching the principles and complex research techniques required of the sophomore and senior in his chosen field or major.

Our first step in the development of our instructional programs was the formulation of behavioral objectives which describe the kind of behavior a student is expected to perform as a result of receiving the instruction. Without such objectives, it would be difficult to determine what to measure in the evaluation. Detailed discussion on how to write such behavioral objectives may be found in my articles in *Drexel Library Quarterly* and *College and Research Libraries.*

After writing behavioral objectives we formulated test questions to measure the student's ability to perform those objectives. Please note that instruction is not yet written. Instructors sometimes write units of instruction and then ask themselves: "Now! What shall we test?" Frequently, they end up sampling segments of instruction which appear to be the most important parts of each instructional unit. We concluded that if a concept was not important enough to hold the student responsible for, we would eliminate it. Because of that conclusion, we designed test evaluation questions for each objective of the program. If the student could perform only 60 percent of the objectives satisfactorily, how could he be excused for not knowing the other 40 percent unless they were not important. And if they were not important, why teach them?

After we had formulated the objectives and written test questions to measure the student's ability to perform the objectives, the test questions were organized into an empirical "task analysis" examination to determine the difficulty, the order for teaching, and the validity of each objective. The "task analysis" is a preliminary measurement which is not involved with complex scientific techniques. It is administered to a group of skilled subjects (in this case librarians) and to a group of unskilled subjects (the group for which the instruction is being written). The result of the examination is to determine without any prior instruction if the skilled and unskilled subjects can perform the objectives. If the skilled subjects, our librarians, cannot perform the objectives, then either the objectives are too difficult or they have not been properly stated. Should most of the non--skilled subjects, or students, be able to perform successfully any objective, then it may not be necessary to teach that objective. They already know it.

Subject reference librarians served as the skilled sample and an equal number of sophomore students served as the unskilled sample. Three kinds of questions were present in this examination: 1) questions calling for memory recall of a rule, 2) questions calling for finding items in simulated materials or xeroxed pages from selected indexes, and 3) questions calling for finding items in an actual card catalog or periodical index.

In most cases we found that librarians were able to perform the objectives and the students were not. Half of the skilled and unskilled subjects were observed from a distance to determine their reaction while performing the examination with no comment from the observer. This observation assisted us in determining where the student or librarian was frustrated or confused. The remaining subjects were observed at close range often asking them questions concerning their positive and negative feelings about the questions they were answering. This provided us a great deal of feedback which assisted in restructuring the objectives and writing the instruction. We were able to eliminate a great deal of intended instruction in areas where most of, for instance, the students already knew the concept.

Remember we are dealing with college students at the sophomore level and often our assumptions as to their lack of knowledge in a given area was incorrect. The best example appeared in the development of our periodical index program. We learned that most of the students were able to determine the meaning of the symbols in a periodical index entry by their own reasoning and except for a very few students such instruction was not necessary. We resolved this problem by teaching the student where he could find an interpretation of such abbreviations rather than teaching him what each abbreviation stood for. Elimination of such unnecessary instruction increased the motivation of the program. Students are not dragged through any more information than is necessary. The result is that the task analysis examination serves as a formulative evaluation for the purpose of justifying the teaching of each objective and refining the objectives to their corresponding test question(s). After a revision of the behavioral objectives and their test questions have been made subject to the result of the task analysis, we are then prepared to write the instructional program.

Several convincing arguments led us to adopt a programmed instruction format for our programs. Dr. M. David Merrill presents in his chapter "Measuring Learning Outcomes" in *Instructional Design: Readings* Page 327, the criteria for a good instructional design which are strongly supportive of programmed instruction and I quote: "A good design continually assesses students ability to perform the behaviors being taught and informs the student concerning his progress. In this situation it is likely that the student may spend as much time in assessment as he does in instruction . . . the pattern is a small segment of instruction followed by testing, followed by another small segment of instruction and so on . . . There is a tendency to think of questions asked during instruction as exercises rather than tests. Perhaps a more meaningful concept of tests in instructional design is to consider all attempts at evaluating a single objective as a single test even though it may be spread over several days or even weeks of instruction. In instructional design the word "test" must be expanded to include any attempt on the part of the student to demonstrate the behaviors being taught."[4]

Another reason programmed instruction was used is that we needed to reach 4,000 students a year and assist them in mastering a large number of concepts. Programmed instruction is individualized and utilizes a mastery of each concept before continuing onto the next. Its individualization permits students to take only the instruction that is needed.

Note that first we have developed our behavioral objectives. Second, we have formulated the evaluation or test procedures. Third, we have developed and administered a task analysis examination and made necessary revisions as a result of that examination. And, fourth we have written our instruction in harmony with the behavioral objectives and their corresponding test questions. Any given segment of instruction then can be traced directly to its evaluation questions(s) and their specified behavioral objectives.

Finally, a summative evaluation is conducted to verify that learning does take place as opposed to other alternatives such as a difference kind of instruction or no instruction. I will refer to the validation of our card catalog program, although all of our instructional programs use similar validation procedures.

Two types of instruction were developed in the card catalog program: 1) a non--programmed version and 2) a programmed version. We wanted to be sure that programmed instruction for teaching the card catalog would indeed by more effective than a non--programmed alternative.

Our Computer Science Department helped us to determine sample sizes, randomization and test procedures, and analysis of data, and our Instructional Research and Development Department conducted the evaluation. Figure I illustrates this particular validation procedure. We used two experimental groups and one control group. The first experimental group received the programmed version of instruction, the second group received the non--programmed version of instruction, and the control group received no instruction. You will notice that three types of examinations were given: a pretest, and two posttests. The pretest and posttest 1 are similar examinations which may be taken in a fixed location and are based upon the memorization of definitions and concepts. The second posttest, however, is an examination requiring the student to actually use the card catalog and is an application of those concepts learned by instruction.

Project: Card Catalog
Validation Procedure

	Pre--test	Instruction	Post--test 1	Post--test 2
Experimental Group 1 Programmed In--struction	x	yes	x	x
Experimental Group II Non--programmed In--struction	x	yes	x	x
Control Group No Instruction	x	no	x	x

Figure I

Both experimental groups received the same pretest after which they were given either the programmed or non--programmed version of instruction depending on which group they were in. They then took the alternative form of the same pretest, noted as posttest 1,

93

after which they took posttest 2 requiring them to make actual use of the card catalog. If the results of the two posttests were comparable, we would be assured that a fixed location posttest might be a possible alternative to the second posttest requiring students to actually use the card catalog. This would be helpful primarily in marketing the instructional package, inasmuch as every card catalog is different. Unless such a fixed location posttest could be utilized it would be necessary to rewrite the posttest for every institution desiring to use the program so that it would be compatible with their own catalog. The third group, or the control group, received the same pretest as well as the second posttest. This group determined the amount of learning contained within the pretest instrument.

One of the main objectives of instruction was to develop an instructional package that would teach students how to find information in the card catalog based on the objective and to do it in a minimal time. Of course, there was no way to guarantee that every student would accomplish this goal even if instruction were valid. The objective was to formulate the program in such a way that if the students followed the procedures outlined, they would be able to perform the objectives in that time limit.

Four hypotheses were tested: 1) The two experimental groups would score significantly higher on the posttests than the control group. 2) The two experimental groups would show significant gains from the pretest to the second posttest and the control group would show no significant gains from the pretest to the second posttest. 3) There would be no significant differences between the two posttests for the two experimental groups. And 4), the experimental group taking the programmed instruction would score higher on the two posttests than those taking the non--programmed version.[5]

Because students signed up for English composition courses at Brigham Young University by English section number and most sections were listed as being taught by "staff," it was felt that a random sample could be obtained by taking three sections of approximately 80 students and randomly dividing them into three groups being tested. According to Dr. Johnson, who spoke to us yesterday, there might be some question about selecting three English classes to serve as a random sample. Additional studies, however, using the "universe" for a sample seem to support the conclusions derived from our original selection. I will refer to those studies a little later in this paper. Two kinds of measurements were considered, the correct responses on the posttest, and the time taken to perform the examination. To avoid the Hawthorn effect, we used a different group in the sample than those who took the task analysis, and no briefing was given as to this experience being an experiment. The only instruction given students was that they were studying a unit on the library. A sumative valuation was conducted over a period of five days. The first day all groups took the pretest. The third the two experimental groups received the appropriate instruction and the control group took the second posttest. The fifth day, the two ex–perimental groups took the first and second posttest.

A one–hour limit was imposed for the test so that if a student failed to complete the test within that time, his test was not accepted. This time criteria was considered important because the–oretically anyone given all the time he desired might find anything he was looking for in the card catalog. This time criterion was twelve minutes longer than the amount of time needed for librarians to take the task analysis test before instruction in which case they scored 98 percent correct. Their student counterpart on that exam–ination scored an average of 32 percent correct in two and one–half hours. If such students could approach the levels of the librarians, they would have demonstrated their ability to perform the objectives satisfactorily. Only two students were unable to meet this time cri–teria.

Results of the data are summarized in Figure 2.

MEAN SCORES

	Pretest (29 ques.)	Instruction yes/no	Posttest 1 (29 ques.)	Posttest 2 (26 ques.)
Group I n=73 Programmed Instruction	9.8	yes	22.4	21.5
Group II n=51 Non–programmed Instruction	9.5	yes	19.2	18.6
Group III n=50 Control	9.0	no		12.7

Figure 2

The mean posttest scores for the two experimental groups were 21.5 and 18.6 respectively. And, the mean score for the control group was 12.7. An analysis of covariance was made using the Scheffe and Least Significance Differences test using the pretest as the covariate. Posttest scores between the experimental groups yielded significant differences both less than the .01 level of sig–nificance between the pretest and the posttest. This was an increase from 32 percent to 84 percent for those taking the programmed in–struction and from 32 percent to 72 percent for those taking the non–programmed instruction. The gain of the control group from the pretest to the second posttest (9.0 to 12.7 or 32 to 45 percent) was found to be non--significant.6

The mean difference between the two posttests (.9 and .6) were found to be non--significant for the two experimental groups supporting the third hypothesis. This was an important conclusion for it suggested that a fixed--location posttest could be used in the published version of the program making it unnecessary for each library desiring to use this program to develop their own posttest. Brigham Young University has retained the departmental posttest because it has felt that there was a reinforcement motivation in actually using the card catalog in locating the concepts called for, and, such a posttest would permit us to evaluate the program continually through computer scoring and analysis. These computer scores could also be routed to the student's instructor and free him from developing examinations for his own evaluation purposes. Our fourth hypothesis was also supported in that those taking the programmed instruction did score significantly higher than those taking the non--programmed version suggesting an important advantage to the programmed learning approach in this study.

Additional studies using the "universe" as a sample showed that all sophomore students taking this instructional program during the first three semesters had average posttest scores between 82 and 85 percent depending upon the semester.

We have found great satisfaction in working as a development team consisting of what we call collective expertise in putting together library use instructional programs which can be shown to guarantee an effective and high--level of learning.

REFERENCES

1. Wiggins, Marvin E. and Low, D. Stewart. Use of an Instructional Psychology Model for Development of Library Use Instructional Programs. *Drexel Library Quarterly* 8:269--279 (1972).

2. Wiggins, Marvin E. An Effective Approach to the Development of Library Use Instructional Programs. *College and Research Li--braries* 33:473--479 (1972).

3. Wiggins, Marvin E. A Scientific Model for the Development of Library Use Instructional Programs. in Sul Lee, ed. *A Challenge for Academic Libraries; How to Motivate Students to Use the Library.* Ann Arbor, Michigan: Pierian Press, 1973. p. 21--46.

4. M. David Merrill, ed. Measuring Learning Outcomes. *Instruc--tional Design: Readings.* Englewood Cliffs, New Jersey: Prentice Hall, 1971. p 327.

5. Unpublished data provided by Charles I. Bradshaw and submitted to the department of instructional research and development, Brigham Young University, Provo, Utah.

6. *Ibid.*

DATE DUE